THE
alternative
BRITISH
ROCK CLIMBING
GILL FAWCETT

Cartoons by
Greg Griffiths

UNWIN
PAPERBACKS

LONDON SYDNEY WELLINGTON

First published by Unwin Paperbacks, an imprint of Unwin Hyman
Limited, in 1988.

Unwin Hyman Limited
15–17 Broadwick Street
London W1V 1FP

Allen & Unwin Australia Pty Ltd
8 Napier Street, North Sydney, NSW 2060, Australia

Allen & Unwin New Zealand Pty Ltd with the Port Nicholson Press
60 Cambridge Terrace, Wellington, New Zealand

British Library Cataloguing in Publication Data

Fawcett, Gillian
　The alternative guide to rock climbing
1. Great Britain – Description
　and travel – 1971 – Guide-books
2. Mountains – Great Britain –
　Guide-books
I. Title
914.1'04858　　　DA632
ISBN 0–04–440114–0

Set in 11 on 12½ point Palatino by
Nene Phototypesetters Ltd, Northampton
and printed and bound in Great Britain by
Biddles Ltd, Guildford and King's Lynn

Contents

Despite their protests
I would like to dedicate
this book to
My Mother and Father

Acknowledgements

Because of the nature of the task I have had to rely on other people to offer advice and recommendations. To this end I contacted many climbing and mountaineering clubs throughout the country to ask for help. Their responses were varied; some were refreshingly straightforward but most were very helpful. From the various replies it was clear that some were formulating their response during opening hours; well done! This cheered me greatly and restored the faith even if the results were completely incomprehensible.

Whilst it would be impossible, or rather possible but tedious, to mention individually the club secretaries and members involved, I should like to thank them for their advice, for seeing the funny side and for entering into the spirit of the thing.

(To Mr H. Thanks for the offer. I'm still thinking about it.)

I have listed references and comments concerning the lesser known haunts in appendices at the end of each chapter. This is because either a) the venue doesn't warrant a full enquiry or b) part of the fun is the exploration so I am merely passing on recommendations to you, the reader, which have been passed to me, the author. I am merely a receptacle through which information may flow, or more probably, be flushed.

Apart from information gathered through the climbing clubs, several people took pity and offered their services for research. Bristol habitué and local expert *Gordon Jenkin* extended a hand, and like a drowning person I grasped gratefully. He undertook to provide information on Avon and Cheddar. Not only that but he rallied his friends, *Matt Ward* and *Nigel Coe*, to research the Wye Valley and Swanage respectively. Good on yer, boys!

Other substantial contributions were seized upon from *Mick Fowler* concerning Dover climbing; from Devon expert *Don Sargeant* and the southern Sandstone area is covered by *Dave*

v

Turner. I appreciate the time and trouble taken by those mentioned here and am glad to be able to share the blame amongst fellow climbers. Those amongst you with eagle eyes may notice the almost irrelevant gaps, South East Wales for instance. I have it on good authority that 'there are no climbers in this area and as such, no climbers' pubs or cafés'. Phew! That's just the sort of comment that would get someone lynched! I'm glad I didn't say that! (For information on the origins of this blasphemy have a word with Tony . . . oh . . . er . . . whatsisname . . . good looking chap . . . hangs around the bar a lot . . . oh dear . . . no . . . sorry . . . it's gone clean out. . . . Well there you go, a local expert speaks out and who am I to question his reason or sanity?)

Finally I would like to mention the friends who travelled, climbed and 'researched' with me, without whom this book would have been finished in half the time.

Relevant names, in a particular order, include:
Billie, who can be a real dog but is nevertheless faithful and true.
Johnson, my staunchest supporter and best travelling companion.
Chris, my favourite kid brother and sparring partner, who hassled on my behalf and pointed out the very oldest jokes.
Matthew, a sound and loyal companion, who knows what's important.
Clive, *Tat* and *Sean*, for accompanying me on various forays and providing valuable information on the gent's toilets, which as it turns out would have upped the tone and has therefore been omitted.
Ron, for valuable advice and help and the good bits.
Geoff, for having faith.
John, for striving to express what it's all about.

Finally mention must go to the person who approached me at a crag and, referring to some preposterous wordage of mine, said, 'I laughed out loud.'
Cheers! You made my day.

Acknowledgements

Apart from pub landlords and landladies, climbing club members and climbing wall managers, there are several individuals who gave me useful information; they are:
John Beatty, Geoff Birtles, Nigel Coe, Sean Coffey, Martin Crocker, Roland Edwards, Andy Fanshawe, Ron Fawcett, Finn, Greg Griffiths, Gordon Jenkin, Sally Johnson, Chris Kent, Daddy Kent, Ian Lonsdale, Dave 'Goodtime' MacInnes, Bob Moulton, Matthew Podd, Don Robinson, Neil Travers, Terry Tullis, Matt Ward, Paul Williams, Roger and *Chris Whitehead* and anyone else that knows me.

On the graphically creative side special thanks must go to *Neil Travers* for drawing the maps and, of course, to *Greg Griffiths* on whose artistic talents I expect to be able to retire to the South of France quite soon.

And to you, the customer, I hope you enjoy using this guide. If I have inadvertently omitted your favourite place, well, it'll be your little secret won't it?

The Philosophy

'Oh Yeah'

VAN MORRISON

My reasons for setting out on this mammoth task are simple. I have felt very deeply for some time that the climbing world is losing its way. People are preoccupied with technical grades, new routes, publicity, and self promotion. Not everybody, of course, certainly not you or I, but quite a few. This seems to have come about for several reasons; for example, the elevation and subsequent attainment of hero status via the magazines, the realization that recognition can be translated into hard cash through manufacturing sponsorship and the growing band of devotees who regard climbing as a way of life rather than as a jolly old time, dedication sometimes breeding a lack of vision.

For whatever reasons, rock climbing has changed quite dramatically over the last decade. Gone is the popular image of the top rock climber as a hard drinking, loose living party goer, outraging contemporaries till dawn and then climbing at the highest standards of the day. It may seem strange that that situation ever came to exist, it's hard to imagine Said Aouita boogying on down until morning and then smashing a couple of world records. Times had to change.

After the helluva good time had in the Sixties, the Seventies brought a new serious approach to rock climbing. Climbers trained and standards shot up. This new

1

breed of 'rock athlete' had a different image; athletic shorts and vest, whilst aiding free and easy movement, also showed off the body beautiful, muscular, lithe and sleek. Climbers felt good about their bodies, some looked pretty tempting too.

One major difference today is that a high profile can equal money, hence an emphasis on publicity and self promotion. Whilst this might seem initially unhealthy and alien to the sport, there's another side to the coin.*

At the time, 'innovations' such as training, chalk and bolts were greeted with either open arms or derision, depending on where you stood. It is unarguable however that all have helped raise the technical standards for many climbers. Possibly this latest wave of self aggrandisement will have the same knock-on effect. Confidence and determination are essential tools for all aspiring rockers. You will find the epitome of today's top rock jock at the in vogue crags, confident, determined, and about as sociable as a dead ferret.

Admit it, they're not very cheerful are they? I thought the whole thing was supposed to be fun. What ever happened to good old fashioned camaraderie and the spirit of the brotherhood? Not the silly handshake brigade but love of humanity, of one's fellow man. Oh, the joy of experience shared! Friendships forged 'on the rope'! A togetherness and mutual understanding . . .

There's something very satisfying about observing a closely knit partnership working harmoniously on the crags:

'When I say "Take in", I mean TIGHT!! You dozy twit!'

To preserve this great sense of comradeship, the very backbone of British climbing, we must stand firm and say 'no more' to the angry young men and women, the half pints of orange-juice band, the vegetarians, the non-

*Who's kidding who?

smokers and other spoilsports. We must get together and talk about climbing in a proper 'Ho ho, guess what I fell off today!' fashion.

And where is the melting pot, the meeting place for all this sociability and affability? Certainly not dashing between rain showers from one wet greasy crag to another. No! Never! In order to find that sense of well being and goodwill to all men you have to be prepared to spend much time in those establishments known as Public Houses; one of the truly great British institutions. It's hard work but persistence pays dividends. Or between opening times try the cafés. At a push you can try the climbing walls, at least most are dry and warm. To this end, to help preserve our noble game, I have gathered information, at great personal sacrifice, from various meeting places around this great country of ours, er England and Wales. (It's well known that Scotland and Ireland are massive watering holes and as such, they are omitted. I mean, come on, there's a limit and I'm malfunctioning on one kidney already.)

To conclude, I hope you will find here a store of suggestions for whiling away the wet hours with fellow climbers, establishing and reaffirming relationships, thus promoting a sense of belonging and oneness in our fraternity which must ultimately benefit the sport. That's what it's all about, isn't it? And if I catch anyone using the paper as a substitute for something else, there'll be trouble!

So I hope the seeds of my simple, humble, and completely selfless dream have not fallen on fallow ground. My aim is in the interest of higher things and anyone that says this is just a cheapskate way of getting drunk in as many pubs as possible on someone else's money is completely out of order, no way, honest, I swear on my wallet which, oh dear dear . . . must have left it at home . . .

The Method

During my travels in search of data, I tried to visit as many establishments as possible, not that I was refused entry to many but sometimes it all got too much. For the past twelve months I have suffered greatly from a curious form of recurring headache, bouts of morning sickness and a swelling abdomen. This points to one of two things: either I have been taking my research duties too seriously and drinking too much (perish the thought!) or I am about to give birth to some creature whose gestation period is one year. (I have always thought Nelly was a nice name for an elephant.)

However, despite the occasional hiccup, I travelled the length and breadth of the country, sometimes venturing out of the Peak District to such exotic locations as Llanberis near North Wales. In many of my forays I was accompanied by my faithful old retainers Johnson and Bill. What a cheerful trio we were, bedding down in the back of the Bedford, nestled between ropes, empty beer cans and sweet smelling doggy blankets.

Surprisingly there were only a few minor 'incidents'. Settled for the night on the Kirkstone Pass in the Lake District, the two women gazed thoughtfully towards the outline of a hill. Bill gazed thoughtfully towards a small rotting rabbit, Van Morrison sang quietly behind, a mug of red wine served at van temperature, a smoke and we were happiness bound. Ten minutes of peace were crashed by the outrageous dazzle of headlights, main beam. Two men, well drunk, approached us. One knocked on the car window. 'Oh God,' I thought, 'this is it, there's going to be trouble.' It was the moment I'd always feared. There we were, two women half undressed in our sleeping bags, one old van, the gear packed around the seats to make a fast getaway impossible. We were easy prey. One man gestured to me to open the window. 'Play it cool,' I thought. Gingerly I opened the window half an inch. 'What?' I asked. He pressed his face to the crack and slurred, 'Can I put this in for a few minutes?' 'Here we go,' I thought. 'He's going to show me his willy.' Instead he held up a small Jack Russell terrier. Right on cue, Bill leaped from the back of the van, teeth bared, snarling and doing Doberman impressions. I was taken aback. At this point I usually reassure visitors with, 'Oh no, she's only saying Hello, it's O.K.' Although only of medium size, Bill can pack a mean growl. 'Go for it girl,' I willed. 'Sorry mate, no room.' He backed off, leaving us none the wiser as to why, if it were not merely an excuse to gain entry to the inner sanctum, he should want to leave his dog with us. Maybe he was fed up with it. Bill's reward for her faithful service? Five minutes sniffing at the rabbit corpse and a Doggy Choc. Aah! Canine bliss. . . .

Research Method

Having established 'why', it only remains for me to fix the method – the 'how' – of this quest, before plunging into the heart of the matter, 'where'.

The Pubs
I took it upon myself personally to visit as many establishments as possible and gather the information I thought necessary:

1. The name and address of the pub, with a telephone number and directions, where applicable, to find it.
2. The name of our good landlords and landladies, Mine Hosts.
3. The brewery to which the pub is tied.
4. Whether food is served and between what times. Here I refer to the period between 11.30 a.m. and

3.00 p.m. as 'dinnertime' because that's when you eat your dinner. (Outdoor folk with hearty appetites eat 'dinner' not 'lunch'. 'Lunch' is what business people eat.) An example of the cheapest and most expensive dishes offered and whether vegetarians are specifically catered for.

5. What facilities the pub offers; with particular reference to the presence of a dart board, pool table, juke box, games room and public telephone.
6. Are you allowed in with your dog, your children, or your muddy boots?
7. Is there a separate room for climbers? (Enforced segregation?)
8. Is there any overnight accommodation at the pub? Or camping nearby? Or a barn for dossing?

At the end of all this, if I have visited in the flesh, I give a completely honest opinion of the place. I try to be as subjective and biased as possible. This piece is contained under the heading Opinion.

Where I have relied on other people's references, I have indicated this under the heading Comments. These have got nothing whatsoever to do with me and while I must protect my sources I am more than willing to point the finger in an accusatory fashion should the need arise. So Mr B from Matlock will probably be banned from the Stoat and Gynaecologist for describing the beer as crap and the landlord's wife as a 'right little goer'.

The Cafés

The cafés included have information relating to opening times and services offered. Although certain cafés such as Pete's Eats in Llanberis or Grindleford Station café are well known as focus points for outdoor folk, other useful establishments are included, which may not be well recognized but comply with the unwritten standards; reasonable value and basic facilities.

The Climbing Walls

If you are still keen for exercise, despite the weather, you may need to head for the climbing wall. There are over 200 in this country and standards vary from rubbish to very good. I have included information on those that are recognized as being worthwhile. This was supplied by the management of each wall and covers a number of points:

1. The name, address and telephone number.
2. Directions on how to find the wall.
3. Entrance fee.
4. Restrictions on use and any regulations that are in force.
5. Some basic information about the wall itself, the construction, design and year of building.
6. The existence of useful services such as changing rooms, showers, weight training and refreshments.

Although the information included here has come directly from the wall management, it is worth remembering the wall scene is a rapidly evolving one and information can soon be outdated. (My excuse anyway.) What could once be regarded as a high quality wall, and consequently popular, may become polished and worthless after a time.

On a more sinister note, keep one eye on the regulation board. The battle cry might now be, 'Look out! The lawyers are coming!' As legislation takes an ever firmer grip round the throat of many climbing walls, you will come up against rules not mentioned here. What a bummer! Enjoy your sense of anarchy while you can, they *are* coming.

The Aim

We must put British climbing back where it belongs – in the pub. Let's quaff!

An appraisal of the symbiotic relationship between the traditional public hostelry and the sport of mountaineering with particular emphasis on the social interactions found therein

'For this relief much thanks'

HAMLET

Let's face it, we all like to get sloshed. I know I do. And the best place is in the pub although you can do it anywhere – in the bus shelter, down the supermarket or behind the bike shed. However, human beings are gregarious creatures, we need and thrive on the companionship offered by the socially acceptable institution – the pub. Where else can you find the comforting touch of an elbow in the ribs, the delicate aroma of sweaty armpits, stale beer and dirty ashtrays, or the friendly call of, 'Haven't you lot got homes to go to? Go on, sod off or I'll set the bread knife on you!' Apart from my parents' house – which isn't commercially viable – the only place to combine the necessary ingredients successfully is the public house.

The association between the public house and outdoor enthusiasts is well known and long standing. Climbers and walkers have traditionally called in 'for a quick one' for many years. After a hard day's cragging or rambling what could be better than to rest weary limbs in some cool, dimly lit back bar, gulping the warm amber fluid and sitting in quiet contemplation of the day's adventures. The soul is filled with a peaceful easy calm, the spirit, worn from so much uplifting fulfilment, can rest. To sit with one's good friends and savour the journey shared, what could be finer? Walt Whitman reflects that.

'I have perceiv'd that to be with those I like is enough
To stop in company with the rest at evening is enough . . .
I do not ask for any more delight, I swim in it as in a sea.'

The brain, tired from over-use, allows the occasional thought to flit through:

'What a wally Dave is! Fancy falling off a V.S.! Getting my best Hex 3 stuck! The old fool had better replace it!'

Although, in times of stress such as five minutes before closing, any pub will do, the outdoor person is attracted to a particular type. Traditionally climbers and walkers are drawn to basic establishments, noted more for their proximity to activity areas, quality of beer, and friendly landlord, than for fine furnishings, trendy clientele, haute cuisine or good cooking.

The Traditional Outdoor Pub

The requirements for a good outdoor person's pub are as follows:

1. It must be reasonably close to the crags or walking area.
2. The beer must be good, although obviously this will depend on your own peculiar taste.
3. The landlord/landlady should be amenable to the occasional quirky behaviour such as traversing round the walls of the lounge bar in crampons, or those games that University clubs are so fond of. The actual game is irrelevant but the final outcome is always the same, everyone gets paralytic, several people will be sick, just failing to make the toilets, and the Entertainments Secretary will be groping the

Traditional Outdoor Pub

Treasurer sprawled across a table. (These are the great hopes of tomorrow. . . .)

4. Closing time? Pubs should never ever hassle you to 'drink up', it's terribly uncivilized. The evening should merely fade to a natural conclusion rather than be abruptly cut off. This 'fading out' may take anything up to a few hours. The best pubs, of course, offer the ultimate experience. The Great British Lock In. This can take place at night or in the afternoon. Afternoon sessions are particularly dangerous, since the doors will only be opened to let the evening revellers in, and there you are, stuck for the night. How many of us are strong willed enough to leave then?

5. Landlords should be friendly but not effusive. The better ones will say 'Same again?' as you approach the bar for a second time.

   Continuity is important. Pubs that change landlords or bar staff are disconcerting. How comforting to see the same wrinkled face on return visits to the Lakes or Wales, like going home to Mother.

6. There should be enough car parking space for erratic manouvering. Life is fraught enough without getting boxed in between a Porsche and a BMW, or more likely between two old Escort vans. The insurance will have run out and they will belong to the local bruisers. The car park at the Helwith Bridge in Yorkshire is an example of a good car park, a vast expanse plus many exits.

   When I was very young my father used to pass on various pieces of advice, gems of wisdom such as 'Never trust anyone' and 'Always back into the spaces in a pub car park'. Both are worth remembering.

Facilities
7. No fruit or space invader machines or anything that

goes 'Beep, beep or prring' or flashes, absolutely not. No way, not under any circumstances.

8. Food will be available at any time, cheap and good value.
9. No elevator music, muzak or piped music.
10. A games room containing pool table and dart board.
11. A public telephone for conveying excuses, preferably somewhere quiet to give the wrong impression that 'I'm stuck in the middle of nowhere, changing the wheel, dear.'
12. Dogs are allowed to wander around and sit on the chairs.
13. Children are allowed in small well behaved quantities. (I am conceding this point as a sop to those climbers with families, although I really can't see why they can't sit in the car with a bag of crisps and a coke, I had to and it didn't harm me, except once when I took the handbrake off. But that was a long time ago and the scars are hardly visible. I have digressed.)
14. Coal fires are a must in winter.
15. Possibly a separate room for Hikers, although segregration should not be compulsory. Here you can eat your own butties, clump around in big muddy boots and sing tunes popularized by Joe Brown and Don Whillans such as the mountaineering version of The Manchester Rambler which is wittily titled 'The Manchester Climber', same tune and quite a few of the original words.

The Rock Climbers' Pub

There is only one extra requirement here and that is that there should be enough room for describing and re-enacting moves:

'I put my hand up here, then I did this with my heel, clenched my buttocks tightly and smeared off this dinky, and laywayed through and finally managed to buckle my harness up . . . then I got on the rock and . . . blah . . . blah.'

Only 143 moves to go, and each one occupying several minutes of gymnastic explanation; my goodness! going down the pub with your mates can be an exhausting business.

The Proper Pub

'Life isn't all beer and skittles: few of us have touched a skittle in years.'

The Proper Pub is an offshoot of the Outdoor Pub offering fewer facilities but concentrating fully on those available – a particular character and atmosphere in which to enjoy drinking beer. Outdoor types usually like Proper Pubs.

A pub is defined as a Proper Pub if it fits the following description:

On entering the bar the monosyllabic grunts masquerading as conversation cease as all heads turn to stare. It is deathly quiet. The silence is only broken by the odd clink of beer glass on dentures, the occasional shuffling of feet and your embarrassed attempts at conversation:

'Well, it is a lovely day, not bad really for this time of the year, could be a bit warmer but we can't complain, musn't complain really, I suppose, well it is a bit chilly, it's . . . a . . . bit . . . er . . . chilly . . . er . . . A pint of bitter please.'

Silence. Game over. You lost so retire to a corner. The only consolation is watching someone else fluff their lines.

Climbers' Pub

Once the excitement generated by a new face has faded, the room returns to normal. The blokes lean against the bar, their shirt sleeves slowly absorbing the slops. Sid, Mine Host, stares glumly at a plastic Coat of Arms inscribed with the message: 'El Restaurante Expectaculo! welcomes SID AND FLO to Benidorm 1964. Travel with Tranters Tours for Fun! Fun! Fun!' A Flamenco doll which doubles as a matchbox holder sits below as a reminder of Sid and Flo's happy holiday. Down one side of the bar serious competition is under way. It's Dominoes night, and the comforting click is not that of the pool table, but of the bones of the Dommys.

The backdrop will change from pub to pub but some things stay the same.

1. The beer is excellent.
2. The landlord or landlady is dead miserable with a face like a dog's bum. Locals are always served before visitors.
3. Only crisps are available because 'it's a pub not a flippin' eatery'.
4. Dogs are welcome, in fact more welcome than you.
5. Children are not welcome.
6. There are no new fangled gadgets such as juke box or public telephone. Nothing is permitted to disturb the blanketing silence.
7. A coal fire blazes all year round.
8. 'Time!' is never called, clients merely drift into the night, slump under the table or fall asleep in the toilets.

It is a far cry from the all purpose, multi-functional modern pub, more akin to an amusement arcade than a traditional pub. Here in the Proper Pub, the establishment serves one purpose only, the appreciation and excessive consumption of beer.

The Peak District

'I sing the body electric
The armies of those I love engirth me and I engirth them
They will not let me off till I go with them, respond to them
And discorrupt them and charge them full with the charge
*   of the soul'*

WALT WHITMAN

'If I am well oiled I shall soon be alright again'

THE TIN MAN TO DOROTHY

The Peak District is an area of outstanding natural beauty,
approximately 560 square miles of moorland, heather, gritstone and limestone dales. A place of contrasts, cleverly
designed to avoid all the offensive bits, such as quarries
and other places of employment. Have you noticed how
the National Park boundary does a quick spin-around
when it approaches Buxton? Mind you I'm not surprised.
If I didn't live there myself, I'd think twice about going. It
is very handy, though, for crashing out after, or preferably
before, the BMC conference.

The Peak District is situated right bang between Manchester and Sheffield and is consequently very popular
with poor people for whom a day out in the country is a
real treat. I am reliably informed that the downtrodden
masses all catch the train to Edale on Sunday mornings, to
ramble cheerfully through the Kinder mists, visibility
zero, singing spirit-lifting tramping ditties, such as 'The
Manchester Rambler', or, for a refreshing change,

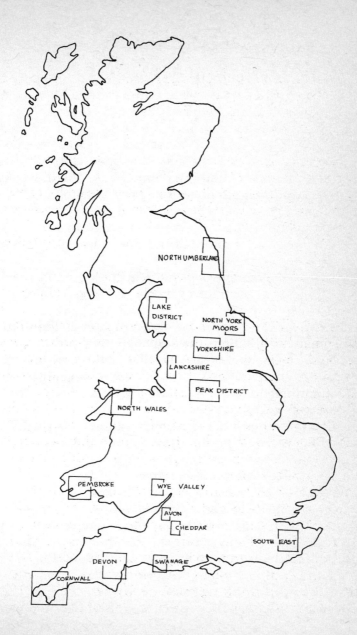

NORTHUMBERLAND

LAKE
DISTRICT

NORTH YORK
MOORS

YORKSHIRE

LANCASHIRE

PEAK DISTRICT

NORTH WALES

PEMBROKE

WYE VALLEY

AVON

CHEDDAR

SOUTH EAST

DEVON

SWANAGE

CORNWALL

'The Sheffield Rambler'. Ramblers are cheerful souls with ruddy smiling faces, damn big boots and flipping great rucksacks.

It's a small-known fact that between 96 and 107 per cent of the whole population live within travelling distance of the Peak District. Small wonder then that Stoney café gets so busy on a Sunday morning. The Peak District is a focal point for outdoor types. The flat vacant spaces are good for rambling over, and the small knobbly tricky bits are interesting from the climbing point of view. All the rocky bits (the technical term is crag) are very close to the road – the A6, in fact – which enhances the attraction of the area for rock climbers who are unable to walk further than 200 yards without activating a condition known as Moan, Moan, Moan . . .

All rock climbers live in either Manchester or Sheffield. To be completely accurate, every climber lives in Sheffield except Douggie 'If in doubt, run it out' Hall who doesn't. Whereas rock climbers, in general, live in and around the Peak District, Rock Stars, in particular, live in communal houses, known as Dosses, in Sheffield. They usually cohabit in groups of about four to six in squalid conditions and pretend to be 'technical advisors' to equipment manufacturers.

Here is an excerpt from a conversation I overheard. I shall simply refer to the climbers as Julian and Stu.

'Ooh, who's pinched my hairdryer, I'm doing the new FAECES ad tomorrow. What do you think of this? I'm going to go all in mauve with a DA and a quiff. Is it me? Julian, are you listening to me? Stop playing with it! Now, where on earth are my new split-crotch, star-spangled, botty-pinching designer sunglasses? How can I do my best and give of my all without them? Oh, Stu, listen love, they're doing me with the new "Outdoor Lifestyle Pack" . . . What? . . . Oh no love, it's a

completely new concept in colour co-ordination. Yes, it is really just a rucksack which clashes with just about everything. Lord, I nearly fell off my slingbacks when I saw it, it's me, it really is!'

(And guess who is paying, indirectly, for this?)

Starting out

Having decided that climbing is the sport for you, you will have to decide what sort of rock to climb on. Basically there are four types to choose from in the Peak District: bumblie gritstone, hard gritstone, bumblie limestone and hard limestone.

Gritstone

'A good gritstone climb calls for the best and most graceful in balance and skill, and the sport is one which should be encouraged.'
WILLIAM T. PALMER, *Odd Corners in Derbyshire*

If you want to be a Rock Star, then gritstone is the rock on which to serve a solid apprenticeship. It is hard and dark, unforgiving and uncaring. Any climb more than HVS is impossible, as there are no holds and you will have to cheat by using techniques (see any instruction manual for further explanation as it's no good asking me, I haven't got a clue). Anybody who tells you that brains, cunning and subtlety are needed is merely being facetious – look at Johnny Dawes; living proof that lack of dress sense is of no importance. Actually there is only one technique necessary to master the classic climbs –

Jamming
Jamming is jolly hard to do. Having selected the crack you

Soloing Peak Gritstone

want to ascend, place a limb into it, then make a fist. Having done this, twist the limb through 360 degrees until there is no skin left and blood is pouring down the crack, all the time saying: 'Oh my God, it's slipping'.

If the pain is unbearable, you can beat the rock with your free hand, using the fist you have already made. (Remember the fist? I imagine you were wondering where that came in.) You can give vent to the inevitable agony through forceful verbal expression, swearing loudly and so on. It won't do any good whatsoever, but it will give onlookers a laugh.

Limestone

> *'Keep off the limestone rocks, novice; they can teach you nothing, and the style of scrambling is dreadful to watch.'*
> WILLIAM T. PALMER, *Odd Corners in Derbyshire*

Limestone is the other type of rock available for falling off in the Peak District. If, as you fly through the air, you wonder why you haven't hit the deck after three seconds, then you must be climbing on limestone. It's the tall white stuff which pops up in several places around Derbyshire. It looms large and frightening at Raven Tor, proudly impressive at High Tor, dirty and slimy at Stoney Middleton, pretty at Dovedale and hardly at all at Pic Tor.

How to be a Rock Star – Peak-style
Many of the keen young leopards follow the standard path to stardom, which is:

1. Go to Sheffield.
2. Go to university.
3. Do not pass first year exams.
4. Sign on.
5. Train like a maniac, become lithe and muscular.

6. Practise sulking.
7. Compile a photographic portfolio, and for goodness sake, no smiling.
8. Become sponsored by a manufacturer.
9. Enter first part of manic depression.
10. Hey presto! Stardom!

There is of course 'The Hard Way' –

1. Be a better climber than everyone else.
2. Hey presto! Stardom!

Bumblie Grit and Hard Grit

The distinction between bumblie gritstone and hard gritstone depends not on the rock but on the attitude of the climber. Bumblie gritstone is any grit climb where the person employs ropes, and hard grit is solo. There may be a few flaws in this definition; Masters Edge, London Wall and others become bumblie climbs and any soloing at Birchen Edge qualifies for hard climbing. (Now this is true! Here are found the most polished grit Diffs in the world!)

The most popular gritstone edge for bumbling on is:

Stanage

No matter how badly you climb, there is always someone worse and the chances are that they will be at Stanage. So don your furry breeches with the sagging knees and the EBs bought two sizes too big to accommodate three extra pairs of socks for winter climbing, grab a handful of ankle bashers and get posing. Posing is like climbing, only better, as you can do it in complete safety on the ground. Posing is all about getting noticed. As a novice, here are some hints. The Equipment Pose: select several of your largest nuts, wave them in the air shouting, 'Hey girls, look at these!', or try the Clothing Pose: tantalize the women, and possibly a few of the chaps, by wearing your pile sallopettes half undone, revealing that macho tartan shirt. If no one notices, you might have to climb to attract some attention. A good ploy is to kick all the runners out, start shaking and shout, 'Oh my god I think I'm going to die'. If this doesn't work, then it will be because someone else has beaten you to it round the corner. You'll just have to shout louder. For goodness sake, don't fall off, having guts is one thing, showing them is another.

Stanage has a well-deserved reputation for Tradition and History. It is still possible to see people placing runners and leading on sight. Apparently Stanage is 24 miles of perfect gritstone with 3,000 classic V. Diffs, so if you must climb then it's worth a visit. On a clear day, there is an excellent view of Castleton cement works.

Stanage is popular with novice hang gliders and parachutists. Lesson One is 'Emergency Procedure in Case Of Equipment Failure'. Anyone observed leaping from the cliff top in the emergency position, i.e. feet together, knees bent and arms flapping, is merely rehearsing for the day of The Disaster. Most get away with it, too, which indicates the height and seriousness of the climbing here.

Raven Tor

This is where all the HARDEST BESTEST ROUTES IN BRITAIN are made. Someone once said:*

> 'Access to the crag is so good that falling rocks will hit your car. Avoid the path directly behind the layby; it's steep and muddy. The one further right is better for the tight trousers and high heels favoured by today's top climbers. Having ascended the path, the potential for

* Me actually.

posing is limitless. *Changing into sequinned dance tights will draw gasps of admiration from passersby. Ignore hecklers who cast aspersions on your sexual preferences. (These people have no sensitivity and would mock Rudolph Nureyev. Mind you, he is getting on a bit and his pliés aren't what they were.) Then some simple exercises to warm up. If it hasn't started raining yet, keep doing the exercises until it does.*

'*Raven Tor is a popular crag and rightly so. It is easy to reach, there are several flat places for sitting and shelter in bad weather. There is only one teensy-weensy prob-lemette – the climbing. Unless you are the sort of clever dick that can get off the ground, it is better to stick to pointing, saying gosh and changing your tights.*

'*One point to note is the shared parking facilities with the fishermen who are usually in close proximity, en-joying a quiet afternoon in the mellow Derbyshire coun-tryside. Rude exclamations whilst climbing will offend them. Other good ways to upset them include sitting on their Volvos or chucking rocks in the river.*'

High Tor

High Tor is the dominating feature of Matlock Bath. A massive wall of limestone offering some of the best climbing around, definitely unsurpassed in Matlock Bath. Access is good and it is possible to drive to the top, parking at the café. Many tourists are drawn to savour the magnificent views of Matlock Bath. It has often struck me as odd that accidents or suicide attempts are rare. As one local resident told me: 'I've lived here for 40 years. I spend most afternoons sitting in the garden and I often cast an eye at the Tor. I've only ever seen one "jumper". I'm pig sick. I've wasted years. I'm off down the roundabout; the traffic lights aren't working . . .' And with that, the cheery old dear hobbled off.

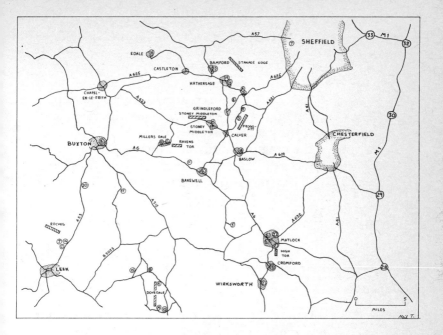

THE PEAK DISTRICT

PUBS

1 **THE ANGLERS REST** Millers Dale
2 **BLACK'S HEAD** Wirksworth
3 **THE CHEQUERS INN** Froggatt Edge
4 **COUNTY AND STATION** Matlock
5 **THE DRUID INN** Birchover
6 **FOX HOUSE** Hathersage Road
7 **THE FROG AND PARROT** Sheffield
8 **THE GEORGE** Alstonefield
9 **THE GROUSE INN** Longshaw
10 **THE IZAAK WALTON HOTEL**
Dovedale
11 **THE MONSAL HEAD HOTEL**
Monsal Head

12 **THE MOON** Stoney Middleton
13 **THE NARROW BOAT** Cromford
14 **YE OLDE ROCK INN** Upper Hulme
15 **YE OLDE ROYAL OAK** Wetton
16 **THE OLD NAGS HEAD** Edale
17 **THE QUIET WOMAN** Earl Sterndale
18 **THE ROBIN HOOD INN** Baslow
19 **THE SCOTMANS PACK** Hathersage
20 **THE TRAVELLERS REST** Quarnford
21 **THE WHITE LION INN** Matlock
22 **THE YORKSHIRE BRIDGE** Bamford

CAFÉS

A **BURBAGE TEA VAN** Burbage
B **DINO'S CAFÉ** Buxton
C **THE EAGLE AND CHILD CAFÉ**
Gradbach
D **THE GREEN SHACK** Millers Dale
E **GRINDLEFORD STATION CAFÉ**
Grindleford
F **HIGH TOR CAFÉ** Matlock
G **LONGLANDS EATING HOUSE**
Hathersage

H **LOVERS LEAP CAFÉ**
Stoney Middleton
I **MATLOCK CHIP SHOPS** Matlock
J **MIDGELEY FARM COTTAGE**
Gradbach
K **MILLDALE CAFÉ** Milldale Village
L **THE PARAKEET CAFÉ** Bakewell
M **THE TEA SHACK** Dovedale

Stoney Middleton

A cheeky little crag this. 1969 was a good year, but it hasn't travelled well into the eighties. It is much favoured by tramps and motorbikers. It is OK to dump rubbish here. Nobody seems to mind. Recent rumours report sightings of the ghost of Proctor, clanking pegs and shouting obscenities at first ascentionists.

The path to the crag is muddy and rocky. Access varies from straightforward, if it isn't your car, to very tricky if it is. Watch out for boy racers in company cars.

Pic Tor

Where?

Dovedale

There is a pleasant dale not too far away, where the trout swim in deep dark pools, where elderly backpackers ramble on well-kept paths, where school children walk in pairs and the birds sing sweetly and nobody leaves litter and the only sounds are the occasional thump as the hard-working Park rangers erect a stout stile or gleaming white limestone wall to prevent disabled people gaining access. In this happy dale no one swears or falls off. For this is Dovedale:

Where the green pool lies the deepest,
Where the grey trout lies a-sleeping
Up the hill and over the lea,
*That's the way for Billy and me.**

Dovedale is a forgotten part of the climbing world. Nobody puts bolts in or wears tights or climbs harder

* James Hogg 'A Boys Song'.

than E3. Not everyone ignores this gem, however. The Authorities are vigilant and tireless in their efforts; things are under control. No place has been overlooked, paths have been straightened, the barbed wire is polished daily and the tree-clearing scheme is ahead of schedule. There are several fine buttresses along the dale, and the tree felling enables the tourists to gaze in wonder at the resulting scree slopes and active examples of soil erosion.

Pubs

THE ANGLERS REST
MILLERS DALE
NR BUXTON
DERBYSHIRE
Telephone: (0298) 871 323

Sometimes known as The Fishermans Friend.
Mine Host is Malcolm Marcroft.

BEER
The pub is a free house selling John Smith's beers.

FOOD
Bar snacks are served at pub opening times.

FACILITIES
These include a games room, pool table, juke box and dart board. Dogs are not allowed in the lounge bar.

OPINION
OK, but watch your language here. A small notice warns that violent words or verbal abuse will result in a ban from several pubs in the area. So be careful, Mother.
 The large car park costs £1 for non-customers.

THE BLACK'S HEAD
MARKET PLACE
WIRKSWORTH
DERBYSHIRE DE4 4ET
Telephone: (062982) 3257

Mine Host is Merv Rogers and the pub is right smack on the Market Place.

BEER
The Black's Head is tied to Hardys & Hansons.

FOOD
Bar snacks are served between 11.30 a.m./2.30 p.m. and 6.00 p.m./9.00 p.m. The menu offers a choice from chip butties at 50p, through lasagne at £1.95 and scampi, chips and peas at £2.25. Vegetarians are catered for.

FACILITIES
Dogs are allowed in when food is not being served. No children allowed, but muddy boots are acceptable. (This sounds like a fine establishment!) Being a small pub there is no overnight accommodation, although several places in Wirksworth do B&B.
   A real fire burns throughout winter – grand!

COMMENTS
'Highly recommended.' Well used by climbers and walkers. 'A warm welcome is offered to everybody.'
   The lack of facilities, attitude to children and so on leads me to conclude that this is a contender for 'Proper Pub' status.
   Most of the climbing population of Derby are here on end of season nights.
   Recommended in CAMRA and the local Derby guide.

THE CHEQUERS INN (Recommended)
FROGGATT EDGE
NR SHEFFIELD S30 1ZB
Telephone: (0433) 30231

Mine Host is Ian Roderick Mcleod. The pub is situated on the main Sheffield road from Calver crossroads below Froggatt Edge.

BEER
The Chequers is a Wards pub.

FOOD
The pub serves both restaurant food and bar snacks between 11.30 a.m. and 2.00 p.m. at dinnertime. Between 7.30 p.m. and 9.30 p.m. only restaurant service is available. Vegetarians are serviced.

FACILITIES
Neither dogs nor children are allowed inside. Muddy boots are acceptable. The pub is recommended in the *Good Pub Guide* 1987 and the *Classic Country Pubs* (CAMRA) guide.
   Overnight accommodation is available through four letting bedrooms.

OPINION
Searching back into the foggy reaches of my memory, I vaguely remember a beer advert on the television depicting climbers leaving the crag after a thirst-making ascent, and rushing down to the Chequers for succour. The joke at the time being that climbers weren't welcome in the pub; this must have been a long time ago as this is no longer the case.

The pub is very jolly and friendly, the atmosphere is congenial and, all in all, a good spot to end a day's cragging. There are only two very small gripes which prevent the pub from being HIGHLY RECOMMENDED. The first is that dogs aren't allowed – surely no decent pub refuses entry to man's best friend? The second is that you often get the GTi brigade in: the types that go to CAMRA-recommended places and talk and laugh loudly, safe in the knowledge that they are earning twice as much as anyone else. As T. E. Brown said 'A rich man's joke is always funny'.

COUNTY AND STATION HOTEL (Recommended)
258 DALE ROAD
MATLOCK BATH
MATLOCK
DERBYSHIRE DE4 3NT
Telephone: (062988) 582188

Mine Hosts are Colin and Pat Bonsall and the pub is on the right-hand side when entering Matlock Bath from Matlock.

BEER
The pub is tied to Marstons Brewery.

FOOD
Bar snacks are served between 11.00 a.m. and 2.30 p.m. and between 6.00 p.m. and 9.00 p.m. Vegetarians are catered for. The food varies from sandwiches at 45p to homemade steak and kidney pie at £2.40.

FACILITIES
There is a public telephone. Dogs are allowed in and children at dinnertime. No muddy boots. Parking is in the council-owned car park opposite.

OPINION
Popular with climbers.

THE DRUID INN
MAIN STREET
BIRCHOVER
MATLOCK
DERBYSHIRE DE4 2BL
Telephone: (062988) 302

Mine Host is Brian Bunce and the manager is Chris Rose. The pub is found by turning off the B5056 (Bakewell/Ashbourne Road) to Birchover, 3 miles from Haddon Hall.

BEER
The Druid is a free house.

FOOD
Restaurant and bar snacks are served between 12.00 and 2.00 p.m. and between 7.00 p.m. and 10.00 p.m. Veggies are safe here. The menu is displayed on a blackboard and changes often.

FACILITIES
Children are allowed in when dining. No dogs. A dart board is proffered for entertainment. Muddy boots are only allowed in certain rooms. There are several boulders, known as Rowler Rocks, at the rear of the inn.

COMMENTS
'Bit upmarket and crowded but the food is excellent.'

FOX HOUSE
HATHERSAGE ROAD
LONGSHAW
SHEFFIELD S11 7TY
Telephone: (0433) 30374

Mine Host is John K. Hayes. The pub is situated on the main Hathersage Road to Sheffield.

BEER
The pub is tied to the Bass Brewery.

FOOD
Bar snacks are available between 12.00 and 2.00 p.m. at dinnertime and, in the evening, from 7.30 p.m. to 9.30 p.m., ranging from sandwiches to scampi and duckettes (?). Coffee is available and vegetarian dishes are served.

FACILITIES
These include a dart board and a public telephone. Dogs are allowed in

the pub, as are children, though only at dinnertime when cooking is taking place. Muddy boots are OK.

The pub is very popular with walkers and climbers. Although there is no accommodation available, it is possible to camp by arrangement.

OPINION
OK, although tends to get very busy at weekends which is only to be expected given the location.

THE GEORGE (Highly Recommended)
ALSTONEFIELD
NR ASHBOURNE
DERBYSHIRE DE6 2FX
Telephone: (033527) 205

Mine Host is Richard Grandgee.

BEER
The George is tied to Allied Breweries.

FOOD
Bar snacks are served between 12.00 and 2.00 p.m. at dinnertime, and from 7.00 p.m. to 10.00 p.m. at night. The vegetarian menu is limited, i.e. a quiche.

FACILITIES
No dogs, but children are allowed in, as are muddy boots. There is a telephone close by outside. There is occasionally a dart board in winter. A caravan site is across the road. The landlord is a pillar of the local community.

THE GROUSE INN
LONGSHAW
SHEFFIELD S11 7TZ
Telephone: (0433) 30423

Mine Hosts are Mr and Mrs Mark Fletcher. The Grouse is situated on the B6054 from Froggatt to Sheffield.

BEER
The pub is a free house.

FOOD
Bar snacks are served between 12.00 and 3.00 p.m. and between 6.30 p.m. and 11.00 p.m. (fairly comprehensive serving times, eh?). Veggie stuff is on offer.

FACILITIES

These include a dart board and a public telephone. Dogs are allowed inside. Children are allowed in part of it, as are muddy boots.

A separate room is available for climbers and walkers and the pub is frequented by many walkers and climbers.

OPINION

OK. Very handy for Froggatt.

THE IZAAK WALTON HOTEL
DOVEDALE
NR ASHBOURNE
DERBYSHIRE
Telephone: Thorpe Cloud 378406

The hotel is named after the fisherman author Izaak Walton who wrote *The Compleat Angler*, published in 1653. Regarded by some to be the father of modern-day fly fishing he is supposed to have had some strange ideas compared to modern fishing ethics. For instance, he recommended eating the fish caught (that seems perfectly sensible to me – what's the point of it otherwise?) and even went so far as to recommend a recipe for pike, a singularly unappetizing dish. (Apple pike and cream, possibly?)

The Izaak Walton Hotel itself is rather a grand place as climbers' and walkers' rest spots go, they even have carpets in the bar. A fine needlepoint tapestry hangs there, depicting Haddon Hall back to front. Try not to spill beer or drop fag ash on it, it must be worth a fortune. Despite the posh interior the welcome of outdoor folk is civil; muddy boots and small muddy dogs are allowed in. The buttery is open from April to October and teas are available 24 hours otherwise, but tea at 80p a pot isn't cheap.

The hotel is owned by the Duke of Rutland who no doubt likes to nip down the dale for a bit of bouldering, in between oik bashing and grouse sprotting.*

The pub is popular on the day of the Dovedale Death Dash which is a 5-mile fell race and attracts many climbers who are old enough to know better.

OPINION

Rather pleasant actually.

* Look it up!

THE MONSAL HEAD HOTEL
MONSAL HEAD
ASHFORD IN THE WATER
BAKEWELL
DERBYSHIRE DE4 1NL
Telephone: (062 987) 250

Mine Host is Nicholas Alan Smith. The Monsal Head is situated at the top of Monsal Dale, up the hill from Cressbrook. From the other side, you turn off the A6 Buxton/Bakewell road, then right through Ashford In The Water, following the signs to Monsal Dale.

BEER
The pub is a free house.

FOOD
Both bar snacks and restaurant meals are offered. Times for serving are between 12.00 and 2.30 p.m. and 7.00 p.m. to 9.30 p.m. Dishes on offer range from a full evening meal to sandwiches. Tea and coffee are served. Veggie types are accommodated.

FACILITIES
These include a juke box, dart board and public telephone. Dogs and children are allowed. Within limits, muddy boots are acceptable in the Stable Bar at lunchtime.
   The pub is fully residential for overnight accommodation.
   Other points to note; the Monsal Head Centre (round the back of the pub) is one of the centres for cycle hire. Tel: (062 987) 505 for details. There is also a craft gallery selling local arts and crafts and books relating to Derbyshire.

OPINION
A large comfortable pub with excellent views down the dale, much changed from the days when Tuesday night was rock night, the head-banging music proving a focal point for rockers, bikers and other dubious factions – bye 'eck we 'ad some good do's . . .

THE MOON
STONEY MIDDLETON
DERBYSHIRE
Telephone: (0433) 30203

The relationship between The Moon and the climbing world has been split into two distinct periods by the past few years when the pub changed from being in vogue, through an unsuitable period and now it looks as though it may become the popular haunt it once was, with the advent of a new landlord, a kindred spirit. What happens remains to be seen but its past associations with the climbing world are well known.

This was the pub climbers staggered from on Sunday afternoons in search of glory and god up the dale. A session in The Moon followed by an afternoon's cragging; several notables ended up in hospital as a result. There were shaky solos; people falling backwards off Windy Ledge; new routes climbed with up to 18 first ascentionists and climbers going walkabout for days at a time. All this has changed, leaving the pub half cut is no longer the guarantee of instant fame as a hard man and good climber that it once was. But they were good days. The Moon was 'The' place to go. All the Beautiful People of the climbing world gathered there. Peggy was the landlady then, and ruled the pub with a firm hand. If you were in favour, great, but if not you were out. Bob Dearman once dared to criticize the beer and got banned for his pains. But it was civilized then. The tale goes that the local bobby once pointed out closing time to Peggy. The village applied some pressure on him and his family, and closing time was never mentioned again.

After a good session, those in favour might be allowed to doss down in the pub, and receive a cooked breakfast the following morning. Otherwise it was sleeping in the outside toilets and a mug of tea to start the day. Oh happy times!

THE OLD NAGS HEAD (Recommended)
EDALE
VIA SHEFFIELD
DERBYSHIRE S30
Telephone: (0433) 70291

The pub is found by following the road to Edale from the A6 and is at the far end of the village. The Old Nags Head is very easy to find; it's on top of the Old Nags Shoulders.

BEER
The pub is a free house.

FOOD
Bar snacks are served during the **summer** at dinnertime between 11.30 a.m. and 2.00 p.m. Mondays to Saturdays. On Sundays from 12.00 to 1.30 p.m. In the evenings between 6.30 p.m. and 9.00 p.m., except on Fridays and Saturdays when food is served half an hour later, until 9.30 p.m.

During the **winter** dinnertime hours are 12.00 till 2.00 p.m., except Sundays when it is 12.00 to 1.30 p.m. During the evening, times are 6.30 p.m. to 9.30 p.m. every night except Sunday when it is 7.00 p.m. to 9.00 p.m.

The menu ranges from sandwiches at 75p to Scampi and Chips at £1.95. Salads are available during the summer season* only. Vegetarians are shunned.

FACILITIES
These include a few machines which should be ignored and a public telephone. Dogs are allowed in and there is a family room for children. Muddy boots are OK. The train station is five minutes' walk and the Pennine Way starts here. There are local camp sites and cheap B&Bs close by.

OPINION
A grand pub this. It is very popular with outdoor types – walkers rather than climbers – and gets quite busy and cheery.

YE OLDE ROCK INN
UPPER HULME
LEEK
STAFFORDSHIRE
Telephone: Blackshaw 324

Mine Hosts are John and Hilary Burows. The pub is situated 4 miles outside Leek on the main road towards Buxton turning down the slip road towards the Roches.

BEER
The Rock is a free house.

FOOD
Pub meals are served offering a variety of 30 dishes, so there should be something to please. Times for food are between 12.00 and 2.30 p.m. at dinnertime and 7.00 p.m. and 11.00 p.m. Whoopee! Veggie types are catered for and, my goodness, talk about molly coddling – cheese and onion butties to start with! Food available ranges from sandwiches to T-bone steaks.

FACILITIES
There is a separate room for climbers and walkers, a dart board and a public telephone 30 yards away, so a good aim is essential. Dogs, children and muddy boots are allowed in the Hikers Bar, the entrance to which is round the back.
    Camping is available about half a mile away, towards the Roches.

OPINION
The Rock has been a favourite spot for climbers to finish off an evening's sport at Hen Cloud, Ramshaw or the Roches. However, I am

---

* July 22nd.

always slightly suspicious of any pub that asks climbers and walkers, to use a separate entrance. Even on those rare occasions of family outings or jaunts with non-climbing friends, when I have appeared wearing the frock and war paint, I feel that I may be asked at any moment to vacate the main lounge bar; a discreet tap on the shoulder and, 'I'm sorry, Modom, but it's no use, we know there's a rope and a chalk bag in your car, so if you'd kindly use the Hikers Bar . . .'

To conclude, the atmosphere is fairly congenial and attracts the Sunday polishers. It is best visited only if you are rushing down from the crag to catch last orders. An alternative suggestion is the Travellers Rest about 4 miles towards Buxton.

YE OLDE ROYAL OAK INN (Highly Recommended★★★)
WETTON
NR ASHBOURNE
DERBYSHIRE DE6 2AF
Telephone: (0335) 27287

Mine Hosts are Roger and Trisha Probert. The Royal is situated bang smack in the charming village of Wetton.

BEER
The pub is a free house serving Ruddles beers, brewed by traditional methods in Rutland, and also the traditional Yorkshire brew of Theakstons. The menu produced by the pub states that 'the malt is mashed with spring water drawn from a well sunk deep beneath the brewery and an old variety of hops, called Fuggle are used'. So now you know.

FOOD
Bar snacks are served between 12.00 and 2.00 p.m. every dinnertime except Sundays, when it is from 12.00 to 1.45 p.m., and in the evening from 7.00 p.m. to 8.30 p.m. The menu is comprehensive including vegetarian dishes, and ranges from sandwiches to duck à l'orange. Tea and coffee are also available.

FACILITIES
A dart board is in operation; dogs on leads are allowed in. Children are allowed in the sun lounge only. Muddy boots are acceptable.

Large numbers of climbers and walkers use this pub. There is also a separate room available for people wishing to eat their own food, although advance booking is advisable.

Camping is available behind the pub and bunk-house-style facilities are situated in a stone building, although advance booking is advisable.

The pub is recommended in the *Good Food Guide* and the *Good Beer Guide* – and now for the kiss of death! . . . this one.

NB: I have to say that it was here, many years ago, that I was introduced informally to the quaint old Derbyshire village sport of Dwyl Flunking. The game consists of two teams, one, holding hands, dancing or skipping in a circle around one member of the opposing team. This person has a stick, a cloth and a bucket of slops. The cloth is soaked in slops and thrown, using the stick, at the circle of dancers. Whosoever the cloth hits is obliged to drink a pint of beer in one; any remaining in the glass is poured over the head. All the beer is provided free by the pub and a merry afternoon's entertainment is had by all.

THE QUIET WOMAN (Highly Recommended★★★)
EARL STERNDALE
NR BUXTON
DERBYSHIRE
Telephone: Longnor 211

Mine Host is John Mellor. The Quiet Woman is found by turning off the Buxton/Ashbourne road at Brierlow Bar and then about 2½ miles past Peakstone Quarry to the small village of Earl Sterndale.

BEER
Marstons.

FOOD
Bar snacks are served at lunch time and early evening, with vegetarians left wanting, and why not? They should eat proper food like the rest of us, not flipping rabbit food.

FACILITIES
There is a dart board, and a pool table in the back room. No dogs (this cannot be so!).

OPINION
Occasionally one finds a pub that satisfies all the requirements of a Proper Pub; the silence is broken only by the odd slurp of beer, the comforting click of dominoes, the occasional 'Eh up, Jack' as old Jack enters, followed by communal glaring as you realize that the ultimate faux pas has been committed – you are sitting in Jack's seat, better move before you're asked. It's the sort of pub where a friendly welcome has to be earned; there's no effusive gushing here, and the blanket acceptance of the term 'local' extends as far as the village boundary and then only after three generations. But once you're settled in for the evening and have had a few words with everyone, possibly

bought a few rounds, then a good evening's enjoyment is possible.

The pub is quite small. There are two rooms, the back room housing the pool table. Before this gaming intrusion, this back room was similar to the family 'best room'; it didn't matter how busy the main bar was, no one ever used the best room. There have been busy times when, having raised the glass to the lips, it stayed there, and still the back room remained empty.

One major advantage of the Quiet Woman is the proximity to Alderley Cliff, a small limestone crag just down the road. Access used to be restricted (shame!), so you could set off in good faith for an evening's cragging, arrive at the crag and find that it wasn't possible to climb due to the nesting habits of the Alderley Cliff Sparrow which raised the question 'what to do?' Well you could always pop into the Quiet Woman for a half? Well there was no point in rushing off was there? What about another? And there you were, well set for the evening . . . or longer . . .

Nowadays, thanks to the vigilance of the BMC, you no longer have this excuse to go straight to the pub. The best thing to do is pretend you didn't realize the access problem had been sorted out and nip in quickly before objections from keen climbers can be voiced.

THE ROBIN HOOD INN
BASLOW
NR BAKEWELL
DERBYSHIRE DE4 1PQ
Telephone: (024688) 3186

Mine Host is Brian Bakel. The Robin Hood is situated at the junction of the B6050 to Cutthorpe and Old Brampton on the A619 from Baslow to Chesterfield.

BEER
Mansfield beers.

FOOD
Bar snacks are served between 12.00 and 2.00 p.m. and 7.00 p.m. and 9.30 p.m. all evenings except Sunday. Vegetarians are given the cold shoulder, ha, ha.

FACILITIES
These include a large games room, a pool table, a juke box, a dart board and a public telephone for phoning to say you've had a spot of bother with the car and will be back as soon as possible. Dogs, muddy boots and children are all allowed in the Hikers Bar.

OPINION
Over all quite a reasonable place. At least they are well used to climbers and walkers so there's no problem there.

THE SCOTSMANS PACK
SCHOOL LANE
HATHERSAGE
NR SHEFFIELD
Telephone: (0433) 50253

Mine Hosts are recently arrived and are Mr and Mrs Simoniter.

BEER
The pub is tied to the William Stones Bass brewery.

FOOD
Bar snacks up to £3.50 are served between 12.00 and 2.00 p.m. at dinnertime and between 7.00 p.m. and 9.30 p.m. at night. Food ranges from sandwiches to chicken chasseur. Meals sans dead flesh are not available. During winter there will be evenings when food is not available.

FACILITIES
These include a dart board and games room and a public telephone. Guide dogs only are allowed in: children too, although only in a separate room. Muddy boots are not acceptable.

A POINT OF INTEREST
The management gives some information as to the derivation of the pub's name:

> 'Prior to the eighteenth century, there were few roads in Derbyshire. The Scotsmans Pack stands on one of the old tracks leading to Sheffield and Sheffield Manor Castle: it was a regular calling place for food and shelter for the "Packmen" or "Travelling Drapers" who visited every farm and village in the area offering their goods and carrying news – packmen from Scotland sold their tweeds here to local farmers.'

So basically things are still the same; a meeting place for a pint and a gossip.

OPINION
Oh dear, this is a tricky one. Until recently no praise would have been too high. The Scotsmans was well noted for its ambience, conviviality and aura of goodwill to all climbers. However, the times they are a-changing. In July 1987 the pub was done out, trendified and tarted up. It now looks suspiciously like 'town come to country'. Gone are the comfortable tatty red seats, in comes brown plush velour upholstery.

Everything is now of a good standard and you can't blame the landlord if he doesn't want wet dirty people on the seats. It is not the place to go if you've just fallen in a quagmire (once upon a time a pre-pub dip in a filthy hole was compulsory, it was called speleology), or walked through a downpour. Sorry. This is quite understandable, especially with the new carpets. However, those dirty wet outdoor types are not known for abstinence and probably made up 100 per cent of the trade. Oh well, we'll see what happens . . .

THE TRAVELLERS REST
QUARNFORD
NR BUXTON
DERBYSHIRE
Telephone: (0298) 4253

Mine Host is John Beswick and the pub is on the main Leek to Buxton road about 5 miles from the Roches. It is on a sharp bend, making it a good contender for the first drive-in pub in Britain.

BEER
The Travellers Rest is a free house with between 30 and 40 different beers to choose from.

FACILITIES
An excellent juke box, vast selection of beers, good fires roaring through the winter (up here that is from October to Easter and through to October again). The pub is a favourite with bikers, otherwise the clientele is usually made up of locals, which is odd since the nearest house is about 10 miles away.

OPINION
A good alternative to the Rock at the Roches if you're not rushing for last orders.

THE YORKSHIRE BRIDGE
ASHERTON ROAD
BAMFORD
NR SHEFFIELD
Telephone: (0433) 51361

Mine Hostess is Barbara Clowes and the pub is on the left-hand side of the main road from Bamford to Sheffield, about 2 miles outside the village.

BEER
The Bridge is tied to Stones, selling traditional beers.

FOOD
Only sandwiches are available at dinnertime.

FACILITIES
There is a juke box and a bandit machine. A public telephone is about 200 yards from the pub. The big three are allowed in: dogs, kids and boots. Climbers and walkers tend to use the tap room, although there is a snug. There is camping 2 miles away at Bamford.

Cafés

DINO'S CAFÉ
MARKET PLACE
BUXTON
DERBYSHIRE

This is the ex-Clovercrest, probably the best cheap basic caff in Buxton, next door but two to Jo Royles' outdoor equipment shop.

OPENING TIMES
Open seven days a week from 8.00 a.m. to 5.00 p.m. The restaurant part is open from 6.00 p.m. to 11.00 p.m. from Wednesday to Sunday.

THE EAGLE AND CHILD CAFÉ (Recommended)
GRADBACH
STAFFORDSHIRE

Where once operated a pub, now stands a small farmhouse café. It is homely and cosy. Often a coal fire burns to create a comforting womb-like atmosphere. However, it is small and weekends are best avoided. Open all year, but shutting at 5.00 p.m. Tea, scones and things on toast are served in the front parlour. The service is friendly and reasonably quick. The cheese on toast is particularly recommended at 35p per slice. Tea is 25p per pot. The toilet is clean with soft paper.

OPINION
Definitely worth a visit midweek.

THE GREEN SHACK (Recommended)
MILLERS DALE STATION
MILLERS DALE
NR BUXTON
DERBYSHIRE

OPENING TIMES
The café is open six days a week, from Tuesday to Sunday, from 12.00
p.m.(ish) to 5.30 p.m.(ish).

OPINION
A grand little café.

GRINDLEFORD STATION CAFÉ (Highly Recommended)
GRINDLEFORD
DERBYSHIRE
Telephone: (0433) 31011

Proprietor, Philip Eastwood.

OPENING TIMES
During the week opening hours are 8.30 a.m. to 6.30 p.m. and at
weekends from 8.30 a.m. to 8.00 p.m. Closed over Christmas from
Christmas Eve to Boxing Day.

FACILITIES
There is a public telephone, space invader machines, which may or
may not be a plus point, a notice board, a small bar for alcohol, and in
winter a good fire is usually blazing away. Climbing magazines are
sold. Club dinners are catered for, so you can have a right good
all-night knees up and Philip also does a Christmas meal at £7.

OPINION
The café, once the railway station where time stands still at twenty-five
to four, is recommended for a number of points. It is very friendly,
large enough to cater for the masses it attracts, the food is good value
and the menu is extensive, good facilities for parking, it is licensed and
open all the hours God sends. The decor is basic but comfortable and
various climbing and outdoor posters adorn the walls. The atmosphere
is one of hustle and bustle as hordes of cagoules, big boots and
weather-beaten faces escape the rain. A jolly place and well worth a
visit.

LONGLANDS EATING HOUSE
MAIN ROAD
HATHERSAGE
DERBYSHIRE
Telephone: (0433) 51936

This new eatery is found by entering into, and going upstairs, 'outside'
(?) the climbing and outdoor commercial complex masquerading
ineptly as a mere 'shop'. This is almost directly opposite The George
Hotel.

OPENING TIMES
The café-cum-restaurant is open from 10.30 a.m. onwards serving coffee, lunches, snacks and teas, until 5.00 p.m. From 6.30 p.m. onwards the Eating House opens as a restaurant, only staying open until such time as people stop chewing. At weekends it is advisable to book a table.

COMMENTS
Pleasant surroundings but a bit pricey. However, this could fill the gap in the upmarket Peak climbers' café scene. Not everyone likes stewed tea and floating grease, so they could be onto a winner here.

LOVERS LEAP CAFÉ
STONEY MIDDLETON
DERBYSHIRE
Telephone: (0433) 30334

Proprietor, Danny.

OPENING TIMES
Closed all day Mondays. Open between the hours of 8.00 a.m. to 4.00 p.m. Tuesdays to Fridays, and from 8.30 a.m. to 6.00 p.m. on Saturdays, and on Sundays from 8.30 a.m. to 6.30 p.m.

FACILITIES
Food and beverages are served. A notice board for leaving messages, a new route book for insults. Maps, guide books and chalk are on sale. A small shop sporadically appears selling bits and pieces of climbing gear.

OPINION
Together with Grindleford, this is one of the main climbing cafés in the Peak District. It has long been a focal point for climbers; it is easy to hitch to and only a few hundred yards from the much maligned Stoney crag. Whilst both crag and café attract criticism, they are useful wet weather alternatives.

The café derives its name from a tale concerning a girl jumping from the top of the crag to commit suicide at the loss of a loved one. What happened as she jumped astounded onlookers. Her petticoats billowed in the wind and she was carried several hundred yards. Thus was parachuting invented.

The café is small, seating about 30 people at a crush and the done thing on Sunday summer mornings is to stand outside, brew in hand, choking on quarry dust and lorry fumes.

The café is popular midweek with lorry drivers and travellers which says something for the price and quality of the food. You don't find

Lovers Leap Café at Stoney Middleton, Peak District

many truckers at Ye Olde Worlde Twee Coffee Shoppe. The tea seems to be prepared well in advance. The fruit pies are recommended. Avoid the Full Set after a heavy night out. Avoid the toilets at any time.

All in all, a good place to while away a rainy afternoon. (How long can you make one cup of tea last?) Where else can you see famous rock stars cadging cigarettes and squabbling over grades?

MIDGELEY FARM COTTAGE (Worth a Visit)
GRADBACH
STAFFORDSHIRE

A typical farmhouse parlour kitchen, found a few hundred yards up the road from the Methodist Chapel. Tea is 36p and a cheese sandwich costs 80p. The lady opens seven days a week all year round and used to be popular with cyclists until the opening of some opposition (!) a few years ago further up the road (see under Eagle & Child). There seems to be some aggravation between the two establishments. (It's the Battle of the Farmhouse Caffs!) If you want to be served at this place, don't admit to having already tried the other one up the road, which isn't open as often as Midgeley Farm. You may well be disappointed . . .

The café is one of those authentic places much loved by townies. The toilet is awful and the inevitable gauntlet of farm dogs has to be run. This passes as character amongst those who know no better.

MILLDALE CAFÉ
MILLDALE VILLAGE
DOVEDALE
DERBYSHIRE

The café is sited at the northern end of Dovedale.

OPENING TIMES
From Easter to October, the café is open seven days a week from 10.30 a.m. to 6.00/6.30 p.m. In winter from 10.00 a.m. to 5.00 p.m. Open Christmas week and half-terms.

FACILITIES
There are public toilets and a public telephone nearby. The café is small, decked with pine and cosy. No hot meals, but scones and sandwiches are available. It caters mainly for the tourist trade of which there is more than enough. Postcards, tea towels and other memorabilia are on sale. They also sell Anadins (for the hangovers) and film, for photographing it. Muddy boots and dogs are welcome; the service is friendly and prompt. Can get very busy with coach parties of German exchange students.

OPINION
OK, considering.

THE PARAKEET CAFÉ
BAKEWELL
DERBYSHIRE
Telephone: (062981) 2349

OPENING TIMES
The café is open from 9.00 a.m. to 5.00 p.m., although they do stay open later if the trade is good.
It is situated opposite the Bakewell Tart Shop in the centre of town.

OPINION
A good basic café: one of the very few in an area which tends to cater for the green wellington brigade.

THE TEA SHACK
DOVEDALE CAR PARK
DOVEDALE
DERBYSHIRE

This is sited at the southern end of the dale. The shack is run by Graham, an immensely likeable chap who 'lives for the car park'. (The car park seems to be a society of its own.) Graham told me about Bob, the previous car park attendant, who passed over in 1983. A little sargeant major of a man with a shock of white hair, he raised eleven children on his own, working in the car park and muck spreading by hand to make ends meet. (Daddy, dear would you do that for me?)

The shack has been there for thirteen years and is open seven days a week, from Easter to October, all day till he's had enough. Tea at 20p is served in plastic beakers and only sweets are available as the people who come to the dale are 'prepared'. In the winter he is only open at weekends, except for Christmas week when the shack is open from Boxing Day to New Year's Day.

There are no other cafés in the nearby village of Illam and no pubs as 'They are all Jehovah's Witnesses and in bed by 9.00 p.m.' Is this true?

Where to Stay

CAMPING BARNS

In the Peak District there are now camping barns available. They provide simple overnight shelter, like a stone tent and are situated at:

Alport Valley
Nr Losehill Hall, Castleton
Abney Village
Bakewell
Lathkill Dale
Birchover

Anyone over five can use the barns, for £1.25 a night, no dogs, and further information about location and booking can be arranged by contacting Peak National Park Study Centre, Losehill Hall, Castleton, Derbyshire S30 2WB. Tel: 0433 20373.

Tourist Information Centres in the Peak District

EDALE INFORMATION CENTRE
Telephone: (0433) 70207

Situated on the right side of the road from Edale Station to the village.

Opening times: daily from April to the end of October from 9.00 a.m. to 5.30 p.m. From November to the end of March 9.00 a.m. to 5.00 p.m.

CASTLETON INFORMATION CENTRE
Telephone: (0433) 20679

Sited in Castle Street near the Parish Church.

Opening times: daily from Easter to the end of October from 10.00 a.m. to 6.00 p.m. During the winter at weekends only from 10.00 a.m. to 5.00 p.m.

BAKEWELL INFORMATION CENTRE
Telephone: (062981) 3227

Opening times: daily from Easter to the end of October from 9.30 a.m. to 5.30 p.m. (5.00 p.m. in winter. Closed Thursdays).

FAIRHOLMES (DERWENT VALLEY)
Telephone: (0433) 50953

Opening times: open daily from Easter to the end of October and weekends during the winter from 10.30 a.m. to 5.30 p.m.(ish).

TORSIDE (LONGDENDALE VALLEY)

Open weekends and Bank Holiday Mondays from Easter to the end of September 11.00 a.m. to 5.00 p.m. approx.

HARTINGTON OLD SIGNAL BOX

Open at weekends and Bank Holiday Mondays from Easter to the end of September 11.00 a.m. to 5.00 p.m. approx.

For further information write to HEAD OFFICE. The address is:

THE PEAK NATIONAL PARK OFFICE
BASLOW ROAD
BAKEWELL
DERBYSHIRE DE4 1AE
Telephone: 4321

CASTLE MOUNTAINEERING CLUB

Meet in their own clubroom behind the **Rising Sun Inn** on Abbey Lane in Sheffield on Thursdays 8.30 p.m. They also have their own climbing wall.

The Peak Appendix
Pubs

THE CLARENDON ARMS
COVENTRY

Across the road from Kenilworth Castle.

THE CRICKETERS ARMS
BRAMALL LANE
SHEFFIELD

The Peak Climbing Club meet here on Thursdays at 9.30 p.m.

THE FROG AND PARROT
SHEFFIELD

COMMENT
Great beer, recommended.

THE GARDEN CITY HOTEL
CHESTER GREEN
DERBY

Derby M.C. meet here on the first and third Tuesday of each month at 9.00 p.m.

THE HOLYWELL
LONDON ROAD
HINCKLEY
LEICESTERSHIRE

Hinckley M.C. meet here at 9.00 p.m. on Thursday nights.

THE OAK TREE
LONDON ROAD
OAK HILL
STOKE ON TRENT

Mine Hosts are Hilbre and Val Jones, members of the South Cheshire Climbing Club. There is a walkers' section.

THE PEACOCK HOTEL
MANSFIELD ROAD
NOTTINGHAM

The Nottingham Climbers Club meets here on Thursday evenings at 9.00 p.m.

THE ROYAL OAK
STONEY MIDDLETON
DERBYSHIRE

COMMENT
'A good basic pub, with games room, pool table and juke box. Conducive landlord.'

THE WHEATSHEAF
BASLOW
DERBYSHIRE

COMMENT
Good beer (Mansfield 4X) and reasonably priced food.

THE WHITE LION
BIRMINGHAM

On the corner of Thorpe Street and Horsefair.

Mercian M.C. meet here on Thursdays at 9.00 p.m.

THE WHITE LION INN
195 STARKHOLMES ROAD
MATLOCK

COMMENT
The bar food is OK. The Hikers Bar is cheerless, but you can eat your own packed lunches in here. Home ales served.

   Derwent Mountaineering Club meet here on Wednesday evenings about 8.00 p.m.

Cafés

ASHBOURNE CAFÉ
Near Finefare in Ashbourne Town Centre.

COMMENT
A fish and chip restaurant. Good value.

BURBAGE TEA VAN
SOUTH END

There is often a tea van parked in the car park for Burbage.

NB: the food needs treating with some respect. Don't spill the coffee on your ropes.

HIGH TOR CAFÉ
HIGH TOR
MATLOCK BATH
DERBYSHIRE

On top of the crag is a café with bar, serving snacks. A juke box, toilets, etc.

   However, if you go as a climber you will have to pay an entrance fee to the grounds.

   There is also a car park at the top.

MATLOCK CHIP SHOPS

The best chip shop in Matlock is Matlock Green Fish Shop.

Yorkshire

'*The Road of Excess leads to the Palace of Wisdom*'

BLAKE*

Aah . . . at last . . . the place that God was saving all the best bits for, Yorkshire! where the grass is greener, the streams are clearer, the sky holds the whitest fluffiest clouds and the routes are harder. (Or at least they used to be, due to the quaint grading system; routes were either 'easy' or 'hard'. If you could do them, then they were easy, and if you couldn't then they must be hard. Simple!)

Whereas Yorkshire was once considered the backwater of British mainstream climbing, it is now firmly fixed at the forefront of whatever is now passed off as the 'exciting new development' end of things. The old grading system had to go, the simplicity of it was out of step with the modern way of doing things, due to bolts and such like. Now it is possible to fail on a climb and still pronounce it 'easy' because of course nobody fails on routes any more, they merely 'work' on them. I myself have spent several months 'working' on an E8 7b, admittedly I haven't actually left the floor yet but that will come, given time.

Although the climbing scene has been fairly low key, the county still produced a healthy café scene. For example Pete Livesey, he does a lovely egg on toast and his waffles are the talk of the village, and, who could forget Mr and Mrs Bonny Masson who do 'things with chips'. And of course Ron who enjoys eating. It's rumoured that

* This was before Old Peculiar was available.

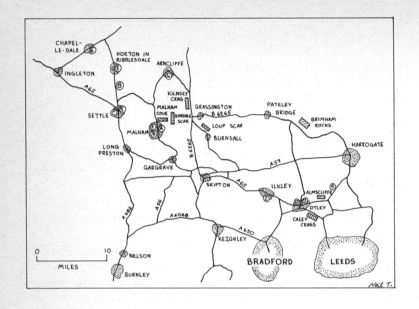

YORKSHIRE

PUBS

1 **THE BUCK INN**   Malham
2 **THE COW AND CALF**   Ilkley
3 **THE CROWN HOTEL** Horton-in-Ribblesdale
4 **FALCON INN**   Arncliffe
5 **THE GOLDEN LION**   Settle
6 **THE HILL INN**   Chapel-le-Dale
7 **THE JUNCTION INN**   Otley
8 **HELWITH BRIDGE**
9 **THE SQUARE AND COMPASS** North Rigton

CAFÉS

A **BECK HALL** Malham
B **THE OLD BARN**   Malham
C **SETTLE DOWN CAFÉ**   Settle
D **TOMMY'S CAFÉ**   Otley

young John Dunne can shift a few mouthfuls of a full cooked breakfast at home, drive to the climbing area and into the café for another cooked breakfast, then off to the crag for three or four E6s, back to the café for a proper dinner before waddling off to the crag for a quick E8, finishing off with afternoon tea to whet the appetite for a good filling tea of double fish and chips, well he's a growing lad.

Apart from their eating habits Yorkshiremen have other notable traits such as the 'short arms and long pockets' tag. Who said that 'A Yorkshireman is a Scotsman with the generosity wrung out of him'? It's true. Have you met the short suffering editor of *HIGH*, Geoff Birtles?

'Hallo Geoff, it's a lovely day, isn't it?'

'Yes it is, that'll be a quid.'

One other feature of the inhabitants is the speech impediment that causes such utterances as, 'Bye 'eck', 'Tha knows' and the completely incomprehensible, 'Ah'm banna ava wesh in yon beck oil' which translates as 'I'm going to have a wash in that stream over there'. This struck me as odd since the person in question had a perfectly good bathroom but there you go.

Despite all this, Yorkshire is worth anybody's time and money to visit. It has dales for wandering through, moors for wandering over and rock for wandering up. The rock is particularly spectacular, the frozen limestone wave of Malham, the oppressive gorge of Gordale, poised to cave in at any moment, and Kilnsey which would be a very good crag if it was the other way up. Apart from the Big 3, there are the gritstone outcrops, hundreds of them, all waiting to batter your ego with their farcical V.S.'s. It's fortunate that, away from the limestone zoos, solitude is easily found and you can flounder for hours unobserved. (I know I do.)

Yorkshire breeds a very strong feeling of pride, nationalistic almost, amongst the inhabitants. It might be something in the water, such as hops, but whatever it is, there exists a dogged, bloody mindedness that Yorkshire is the only place that knows 'owt about 'owt. They might be right. The place is so beautiful, so uplifting that one feels that it must be specially blessed. Big G must have put an asterisk by the name 'Yorkshire' in His bestseller, 'Building the World In Six Easy Days', marking it for special favours. What a pity He was so generous with His meteorological attention; 'WEATHER; Inclement – ominous clouds and driving rain, light drizzles a speciality.'

Famous Yorkshiremen

The most famous son is Dennis Gray. In fact the county is often referred to as Dennis Grayshire* in honour. Dennis is a GOOD SORT and works very hard, in his role as the BMC, ensuring that our freedoms are protected and that women and children can walk the crags at night unmolested (spoilsport).

The BMC do several good things such as considering climbing walls ('Why are they so hard?'), or ecological matters ('Where have all the flowers gone?'), and occasionally giving voice to some deep philosophical problem ('What's brown and sounds like a bell? Answer, dung!')

Many notables attend meetings. Coffee and biscuits are served and excess noise is supplied by Ken Wilson who pretends to be the QE 2 docking in a thick fog. Dennis is usually present to add no nonsense down to earth Yorkshire common sense by saying 'Bye 'eck' and 'eh up' a lot.

The National Officer who is A. Fanshawe can be relied on to say the right sort of thing. Remember the recent Area Sub Committee on Lavatorial Literature? Fanshawe cut through the crap to utter, 'The committee has considered the writing on the wall and found it to be

---

* This is an old Jim Perrin joke, so credit must go to an old Jim Perrin.

disgusting!! Will the person responsible please use block capitals in future.'

The Main Climbing Areas

Limestone

Malham Cove

I once wrote some wordage concerning the delights of Malham and Gordale for *HIGH* magazine. I see no reason to change my mind now so the gist of that article is produced here.

Malham Cove is very impressive. The Park Authorities have done a good job. The crag is in just the right place at the end of the path. Erected signs point out interesting country features such as the stream and the grass. Other attractions include ducks and free-range sheep. This is Mother Nature 'red in tooth and claw' – tamed.

There are three main parts to the climbing arena: the Right Wing, the Left Wing and the middle bit. The middle bit is for the nancy boys to impress the spectators and can be handy for sheltering under. The Right Wing used to be pleasant but someone has erected fences and planted shrubs, and really the Wing has gone off recently. It's hard to believe that student fresher meets are held here now. Whatever happened to Idwal Slabs in the rain? However, the future of climbing at Malham is hopeful and it lies on the Left Wing. Here it is still possible to find pleasing spots to eat your butties, protection against the dements' and the occasional private place for personal intimacies.

Gordale

Gordale, just over the hill, is the antithesis of Malham. Whereas the Cove is open, catching and holding any available sunshine, the gorge of Gordale is dank and oppressive, resisting the fiercest summer heat. However,

if you want to find out about climbing, then Gordale is the place to go. It is guaranteed that within five minutes of arriving in the Gorge, an overweight scoutmaster from West Kirby will tell you, and everyone else within shouting distance, all about it. It's all to do with banging nails in, lassoing trees and Chris Bonington. The Gorge is full of atmosphere which varies from plain dull to downright miserable.

The climbing has been described as 'excellent – steep and technically demanding'. This is certainly not my idea of 'excellent', however for both the climbers in Britain operating at E7, I'm sure a visit would be worthwhile.

There are facilities for camping at Gordale. Enquire at the farmhouse where the path begins. It is a perfect place for camping; quieter than the Malham village site, the gently sloping sheep-cropped field is bounded on one side by a babbling stream, and being a mile out of the village tends to deter the rowdier elements who need to stay nearer the pub, for example, other climbers.

Kilnsey
There are no delights to be found climbing at Kilnsey; it is too hard to be enjoyable. Anyone that says otherwise is either (a) a smart arse, or (b) a very good climber.

Kilnsey is one of the most awe-inspiring and thought-provoking crags in Britain. Why doesn't it fall over?

It is 190 ft of jutting limestone, dominating the surrounding Wharfe Valley. It is in every sense a modern crag: it is multi-functional. You can shelter under the overhanging part, which is all of it, or you can sit in the car, pointing at the crag and causing traffic jams. From a rocker's point of view, the choice of places to fall off is limitless. Although the crag is having to bow to the hard rock climbers using doubtful techniques like skill, dedication and courage, all is not lost. Aid climbers called Duncan still practise their ancient crafts of bolting, pegging and hanging on gear. (Hang on a mo, that's what the hard free climbers do . . . am I missing something here?)

Aah, but the main overhang is still holding out. Now that would be something.

NB: what about facing out from the crag when relieving yourselves, boys? The rain doesn't reach under the over-hanging starts and it's getting a bit whiffy. A small point, but one I feel worth mentioning.

Loup Scar

This is a great crag. It is sited by the side of the River Wharfe which cascades past in cold, frothy whirls. Triffic!

There are only two routes here, both too hard, so you can arrive at the crag, say, 'Oh my god, there's no way', then settle down for a good afternoon. Put the beers in the river to cool, strip off and either lower yourself very gingerly (my method) or dive heroically from the jutting rock shelves, 20 feet up, into the 40 foot dark green pool. Fairly old people should opt for my method unless you want to prove that 'there's life in the old dog yet'.

Try to avoid the place on summer weekends as it gets busy. The best time for solitude would be mid-week in the winter. Take a wetsuit.

Gritstone

Almscliffe

The phrase 'The Yorkshire Wart' refers to this prominent lump of gritstone and not, as is sometimes claimed, a certain Northern lady climber.

Almscliffe promotes a definite attitude, you either love it or hate it. Personally I find that falling into liquid cow pats loses its appeal after the 23rd time, it serves me right for falling off I suppose. But other more skilled practitioners love it. Dennis does.

The advantage about climbing here is that there is no need to specify which climbs you've managed since the phrase 'I've been cragging at Almscliffe' is enough to command instant respect. It's so hard! Ignore the grades. They are designed to humiliate you and confirm the suspicion that Yorkshire climbers are 'dead 'ard'.

Pubs

THE BUCK INN (Recommended)
MALHAM
NR SKIPTON
NORTH YORKSHIRE BD23 4DA
Telephone: (07293) 317

Mine Hostess is Mrs R. M. Robinson. The Buck is sited in the middle of Malham village, 7 miles from Gargrave which is on the A65 Settle to Kendal road.

BEER
The Buck is a free house.

FOOD
Both bar snacks and restaurant food are available throughout opening hours. Vegetarians are OK. Food ranges from quiche to table d'hôte at £7.

FACILITIES
There is a juke box in the Hikers Bar. Dogs and muddy boots are allowed in here and facilities for children are available. There are ten bedrooms and camping in the village.

OPINION
The Buck contains two bars, the lounge bar and the Hikers Bar. 'Hikers' means walkers, climbers, motorbikers and all yobs generally. The chairs are hard bum-numbing benches, the tables are solid, shin-bruising affairs and the floor is bare concrete. Dear, dear, do not we, as honest God-fearing outdoor folk, deserve a few comforts in our hours of need until closing time? And while I'm in whinge mode, the toilets are grotty too. Some sort of conciliatory gesture exists in the form of the juke box, which is excellent and has been described in glowing terms as 'the best in Malham!' Classic rock and pop tunes popularized by dead people from the Sixties play constantly. Great!

COW AND CALF HOTEL
ILKLEY MOOR
ILKLEY
WEST YORKSHIRE LS29 8BT
Telephone: (0943) 607335

Mine Hosts are the Norfolk family. The pub is found by following the signs from the A65 to the Cow and Calf rocks (about 1 mile). The hotel is adjacent to these.

BEER
The hotel is a free house.

FOOD
Both bar snacks and restaurant food are served between the hours of 12.00 and 2.00 p.m. From 7.15 p.m. to 9.15 p.m. it is restaurant service only. Vegetarian dishes are offered. The menu ranges from Dalesman pie to roast duck.

FACILITIES
These include a games room, a pool table and a public telephone. Dogs are not allowed, but children are (What!). Also, no muddy boots.
    The hotel has 3-star accommodation.

OPINION
Well, it is particularly handy for the Cow and Calf rocks, Ilkley Quarry and Rocky Valley if you are rushing to get last orders in. There are pretty views for summer afternoon boozing.

THE CROWN HOTEL
HORTON-IN-RIBBLESDALE
NR SETTLE
NORTH YORKSHIRE BD24 0HF
Telephone: (07296) 209

Mine Hosts are Richard and Norma Hargreaves. The Crown is sited 6 miles from Settle in the centre of the village, between two hump-backed bridges.

BEER
The pub is tied to T.R. Theakstons Brewery. What a lovely prospect!

FOOD
Between the hours of 12.00 and 2.00 p.m. and from 6.00 p.m. to 8.30/9.00 p.m. bar snacks are served. Restaurant service is available from 6.30 p.m. to 7.15 p.m. Vegetarians are catered for by prior arrangement.

FACILITIES
There is a pool table, dart board and public telephone for your amusement.

Dogs, children and muddy boots are all OK here. The pub is popular with walkers and climbers and there is a separate room for them. Hotel accommodation of B&B, £11, is available with cold ham breakfasts for early departures (scrumptious!), packed lunches and flasks filled.

OPINION (completely unbiased)
This is a 'Traditional' climbers and walkers' pub full of people in hairy shirts, 'just up from London'. The sort of pub where people are likely to produce guitars, fiddles and the odd double bass. It is an amazing coincidence that not only will there be enough instruments to play 'Streets of London' and 'Annie's Song', but everyone in the pub knows the words. If there's a pause in the musical proceedings, it's worth requesting the old Leonard Cohen favourite, 'Let's All Go Down Together'. Or try joining in with a set of spoons – the large serving sort make the worst racket . . . er . . . I mean . . . best tunes.

Quite honestly the attraction of this pub escapes me, I'd rather get several cans and sit in my van listening to a few hours' interference on the radio. Much more fun. This has got nothing whatsoever to do with the fact that some bloke got served in front of me, and then, when this was pointed out to the barman, he addressed me patronizingly as 'love'. This has not swayed me one iota, honest.

FALCON INN
ARNCLIFFE
NR SKIPTON
NORTH YORKSHIRE BD23 5QE
Telephone: (075 677) 205

Mine Host is Mr Miller. The Falcon is found by going north on the B6160. Turn left after Kilnsey to Arncliffe village.

BEER
A free house.

FOOD
Only bar snacks are offered from 12.00 to 2.00 p.m. Limited vegetarian dishes.

FACILITIES
In winter a dart board appears. Apart from that you'll have to make do with the public telephone. No dogs. Children at lunchtime. No muddy boots allowed. The pub has twelve places for residents and there is a camp site 1½ miles away.

COMMENT
Much used by outdoor folk and 'highly recommended'.

THE GOLDEN LION (Recommended)
DUKE STREET
SETTLE
NORTH YORKSHIRE
Telephone: (07292) 2203

BEER
A Thwaites pub.

FOOD
The menu is served from 12.00 to 2.30 p.m. and between 6.30 p.m. and
9.00 p.m. The food is good but a bit pricey.

FACILITIES
These include a games room, pool table, dart board and a juke box.
There is a large back room good for do's offering riotous assembly.

OPINION
A grand pub this, although popular with locals. The atmosphere is
very pleasant, with a large open fire and impressive surrounding
fireplace and sweeping staircase. A traditional pub aura.

HELWITH BRIDGE (Worth a Visit)
NR SETTLE
NORTH YORKSHIRE
Telephone: (07292) 6220

The Helwith Bridge pub is sited about 4 miles out of Settle on the road
to Horton in Ribblesdale.

BEER
A Tetleys pub.

FOOD
The pub has a supper licence and meals are bookable to 10.30 p.m.

OPINION
The pub is reassuringly situated out in the middle of nowhere. The car
park is large which is handy for a quick getaway. The landlord offers a
most warming welcome. An open fire and carpets! There is a pool room
and juke box. The menu is reasonable and served continuously. When
questioned about serving times, 'Do you stop serving food an hour
before closing time?', he eyed me incredulously and said, 'What's
that?' An immensely likeable person with basic toilets and soft paper.

THE JUNCTION INN (Worth a Visit)
BONDGATE
OTLEY
NR LEEEDS LS21 3AD
Telephone: (0943) 463233

Mine Hosts are Pat and John Middleton. The Junction is on the main Leeds road in the centre of Otley.

BEER
The pub is Tetley-managed and run on free trade lines, having seven traditional ales including Tetleys, Taylors and Theakstons.

FOOD
Bar snacks are served at lunch times only. Vegetarian meals are also served. The food ranges from a ploughmans to sirloin steak at reasonable prices.

FACILITIES
Entertainments include a juke box, a dart board and a public telephone. Have you ever watched someone trying to make a phone call in a busy pub? 'WHAT? YOU'LL HAVE TO SPEAK UP! IT'S THE TRAFFIC! WHAT? WHAT? OF COURSE THERE'S NO ONE ELSE HERE! . . . I'M NOT SHOUTING!' Very entertaining.
Dogs are allowed in except between 12.00 and 2.00 p.m. when food is being served. Children are not allowed in. (A sensible decision.) Muddy boots are OK as there are no carpets, just quarry tile floor.

OPINION
Some pubs are recommended purely for one outstanding feature; it might be the ambience or a conspiratorial landlord, the food or the situation. Here it is the beer which is simply wonderful. Although the pub isn't a traditional climbers' pub, it is well worth a visit after an evening's bouldering at Caley, or just forget the crag and go straight to the pub. It does tend to get busy, in fact absolutely packed out, but that bears witness to the quality of the beer.
Let me tell you about the beer; it is sheer joy, great gulps of nectar, a treat for the tastebuds. Savour the amber liquid through that creamy head. Pure bliss. It's one of the real delights in life with few equals; blackcurrent cheesecake comes close. A satisfying experience, nearly as good as bonking.
Alternative venue is the Rose and Crown 20 yards away if a seat is required.

THE SQUARE AND COMPASS
NORTH RIGTON
LEEDS
YORKSHIRE LS1 70D5
Telephone: (0423) 74228

It is found in the middle of the village which is off the A658 Leeds to Harrogate road.

BEER
The pub is tied to Bass North.

FOOD
Both bar snacks and restaurant food are served between 12.00 and 2.00 p.m. and between 7.00 p.m. and 10.00 p.m. Vegetarian dishes are served. There is an à la carte menu and 'Farmers Table'.

FACILITIES
A dart board and a public telephone. No dogs allowed and no muddy boots ('but it's not mud, it's . . .'). Children are acceptable. There is no overnight accommodation or camping.

Cafés

BECK HALL (Highly Recommended)
MALHAM
NR SKIPTON
YORKSHIRE
Telephone: (07293) 332

The proprietors are various members of the Boatwright family. Beck Hall is situated on the right-hand side as you leave Malham village for the Cove.

OPENING TIMES
Open seven days a week from 8.30 a.m. to 7.30 p.m.

OPINION
The owners have produced a 'twentieth descriptive leaflet which cancels all others' and which describes Beck Hall as 'pleasant and homely accommodation for those who love the country'. How true!

What could be finer than to sit by a gently flowing stream, tossing crumbs to ducks, sipping tea from a cup, pinky poised, a plate of homemade fancies to choose from, and to be addressed as 'Sir' or 'Madam' to boot? Well, if the sun is shining, you've managed to grab a seat from a touring granny and your attire isn't too disgusting, you might enjoy the treat: it's so English, so pleasant and, more to the point, it's cheap (or cheapish).

Beck Hall is the best café in this area for climbers and walkers for several reasons: plenty of seating, reasonably good value, old fashioned charm and ambience, very convenient for the climbing. On a full day the café may be visited about three times: breakfast, mid-morning and mid-afternoon breaks. More than this is rather indulgent.

THE OLD BARN
MALHAM
NR SKIPTON
YORKSHIRE
Telephone: (07293) 486

Proprietors, Mr and Mrs P. Livesey.

OPENING TIMES
From 9.00 a.m. to 6.00 p.m., and from 10.00 a.m. to 6.00 p.m. in September.

OPINION
Those of you old enough can cast your minds back into the depths of pre-history and recall the name Pete Livesey. He was the one that upset people by being controversial and using Tactics, before it was fashionable. Of course, all this was a long time ago and times have changed. Pete now runs the café and it is not often you get the chance to berate a living legend in his own kitchen on the quality of his scones, which are nice, but chewy.

Although the café is rather small, it is worth a visit, the toilet is particularly pleasant and, if enough money changes hands, Pete will talk to you.

SETTLE DOWN CAFÉ
DUKES STREET
SETTLE
NORTH YORKSHIRE
Telephone: (07292) 2480

FOOD
There is a reasonable choice on the menu which is cheapish, e.g. tea 24p, coffee 37p, full breakfast of bacon/egg/sausage/tomato/bread and butter/toast and marmalade/tea or coffee costs £2.48.

OPENING TIMES
The café is open seven days a week from 9.30 a.m. to 6.30 p.m.

FACILITIES
Flasks are filled, although it doesn't say with what. A notice in the

Pete Livesey's Café, Yorkshire

window gives attention to the hard of hearing. This means that when you go in the staff will talk very loudly and slowly at you. A facility worth noting for passing foreigners which is anyone from outside Yorkshire.

Toilets exist.

OPINION
To be quite honest, the best thing this place has going for it is the name; it always seems to be full of people talking to themselves which is rather disconcerting at first. The decor is Basic Caff but the staff are friendly and if you want somewhere to sit and talk to yourself, this is the place.

TOMMY'S CAFÉ
96 BOROUGHGATE
OTLEY, LEEDS
YORKSHIRE
Telephone: (0943) 462816

OPENING TIMES
Open six days a week from 7.00 a.m. to 6.00 p.m. and Sundays from 8.00 a.m. to 6.00 p.m.

OPINION
A cheap basic café. The food is good value and the service is friendly. The seating facilities are not extensive but, unless a cycling club turns up, there will be room. Worth a stop off.

Tourist Information Centres are at:

Wensleydale Craft Shop, Askrigg
The Post Office, Bolton Abbey
Riverside Gallery, Buckden
The Post Office, Burnsall
Stone Close Café, Dent
The Post Office, Gunnerside
The Post Office, Hebden
Pen-Y-Ghent Café, Horton-in-Ribblesdale
Over and Under (The Post Office), Kettlewell
The Post Office, Langcliffe
Litton Post Office, Littondale
The Village Store, Muker
Swaledale Folk Museum, Reeth
Stump Cross Caverns
The Post Office, Thoralby

For further information contact:

The Information Officer
Yorkshire Dales National Park
Hebden Road
Grassington
Nr Skipton
North Yorkshire
BD23 5LB

Opening times vary slightly, but all are open seven days a week, usually 9.30 a.m. to 4.30 p.m.

The Yorkshire Appendix

Pubs

THE BAY HORSE
BAILDON
BRADFORD
YORKSHIRE

COMMENT
This is the pub for a drink before climbing at Baildon Bank.

THE FLYING DUTCHMAN
SUMNER BRIDGE
NR HARROGATE

COMMENT
The pub for visiting after Brimham Rocks.

THE TENNANTS ARMS
KILNSEY
YORKSHIRE

OPINION
'OK for a break from sheltering under the crag. Coffee served.'

Cafés

BETTY'S TEA AND COFFEE SHOPS
ILKLEY/HARROGATE

COMMENT
There are two 'Betty's' of interest to climbers, one in Harrogate and one in Ilkley.

Betty's is a genteel tea shop aimed at the little old lady market, offering a wide range of teas, cakes and snacks. The service is usually excellent even to the slightly less respectable elements of society – you and me. Comments such as 'I went in wearing my tracksuit bottoms and nobody batted an eyelid' are normal. There must be a limit though. Maybe there should be some sort of contest to see who can wear the worst clothes and still be served decently.

Recommended as a nice change.

THE BUS STATION CAFÉ
SKIPTON BUS STATION
YORKSHIRE

OPINION
This must be the cheapest place in Skipton to obtain food, and as such is very basic and usually full of 'characters'. It was the one place I dreaded being taken to when I was invited 'out' for a meal.

THE CORNER CAFÉ
LEEDS

Sited on the Harrogate Road from the town centre, just past Eric Hunt's car salesroom.

OPINION
Highly recommended curry house, popular with students, lecturers and other economically minded souls.

GRASSINGTON CHIP SHOP
NR SKIPTON
YORKSHIRE

OPINION
'A good chippy, reasonable value, about 7 miles from Malham.'

THE KARACHI CLUB
BRADFORD

Sited behind the National Photographic Museum, the next street up but one.

OPINION
Recommended basic curry house, worth a stop on the way back from the Dales.

THE KASHMIR
BRADFORD

Sited near the university.

OPINION
A basic curry house much loved by students and climbers returning
from the Dales.

Lancashire

———

*'Let us endeavour to live so that when we come to die even
the undertaker will be sorry.'*

MARK TWAIN

This is a tricky one! How to convey my impressions of the
place without offending my friends in Lancashire? It's a
grand place and the people are decent enough but, at the
risk of being banned from that county's shores for ever, I
have to admit that all that springs to mind is how similar
it is to Yorkshire. But not as pretty.

I could comment about 'whippets and flat caps' but is
that Yorkshire or Lancashire? Black puddings? Oh now
that I do know, that's Lancashire! Too easy. But what
about dour expressions, broad accents and the enjoyment
of others' misfortunes? You see how difficult it all is?
Those qualities could relate to either of the two counties.

How peculiar that there is hardly any discrepancy to an
outsider and yet, to the two parties concerned, the differences are diametrically opposed and pronounced enough
to encourage a fight over a bunch of flowers.

Maybe it would be better to concentrate on irrefutable
differences. For a start Lancashire is much smaller, contains the Wilton Quarries and used to host the best
climbing club dinners in the North West (see under Black
Dog Pub). It was at one of these 'dinners' that I first
became acquainted with a charming old Lancashire custom, whose correct title I won't repeat since the word
'arse' might cause offence. However it involves setting

71

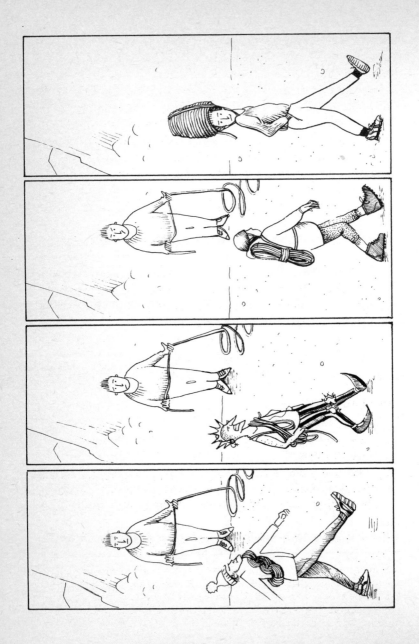

fire to a rolled up newspaper and then running around the room with several friends all shouting 'aagh!' and 'ouch!' It surprised me how active the scene is.

On the climbing side, it is obvious from reading the guidebook and peering through the mists that there are many crags to go at. A Lancashire friend summed it up when out walking in Derbyshire one winter's afternoon. By the side of the path the earth had fallen away to reveal several bands of green crumbling gritstone, not more than 10 feet in height. 'Look' I joked 'a crag'. My pal replied matter of factly 'Oh, Lancashire is covered in crags like that'. He was boasting.

There is one obvious difference between Yorkshire and Lancashire. There are fewer Prima Donna figures in Lancashire. Of course stars exist, like the laconic Hank Pasquill, but climbers tend to be more 'characters' rather than media seekers which is probably the best way of saying the place is full of eccentrics.

Pubs

THE BLACK DOG
CHURCH STREET
BELMONT
NR BOLTON BL7 8AB
Telephone: (020 481) 218

Mine Host is Jim Pilkington and the pub is found by taking the A666 from Bolton to Astley Bridge, turn left at Three Pigeons pub and go straight into the village. The Black Dog is the first pub on the left.

BEER
The pub is tied to Joseph Halls with traditional hand-pulled beers.

FOOD
Bar meals are served between 12.00 and 2.00 p.m. every dinnertime, except Sundays when meals stop at 1.30 p.m. Every evening food is served from 8.00 p.m. to 10.00 p.m., except Mondays. The vegetarian menu is limited. A three-course meal costs £5 and black pudding, curry or roast chicken costs about £2.50.

FACILITIES
There is a pool table, dart board and public telephone. Well-behaved
dogs are allowed and children are OK in the children's room. No
muddy boots. Camping is available in Rivington 4 miles away. The
pub hopes to be offering B&B in 1988. The pub tends to be more
popular with walkers than climbers. Has been recommended in the
Good Pub Guide.

OPINION
This pub achieved fame under the management of Ian Lonsdale who
masterminded the notorious Black Pudding Dinners, an annual dinner
for Lancashire and like-minded climbers at which the Lancashire
delicacy, the ceremonial black puddings were served. Always raucous
and drunken, the dinners were well supported.

However, since Ian has left things are not the same, according to one
source 'it cannot be recommended at all', although the Lancashire
Caving and Climbing Club meets here on the first Tuesday of the
month from October to April at 8.00 p.m. and say it is worth a visit.

(Come on Ian, the climbing world needs these elegant gatherings to
bring a touch of class and glamour to our lives.)

THE CRAVEN HEFFER
INGLETON
LANCASHIRE
Telephone: (0468) 41427

BEER
A Thwaites pub, sited in the village.

This pub has certainly suffered as the whims of the caving world
have changed. Once 'the' pub for the caving scene in this area – the
Moon of the sport – it is now merely a shadow of its former glory. A
change of landlord, a pool table replacing the old piano and bang! all
that lovely business gone.

FOOD
The chocolate fudge cake is yummy and will leave you feeling pretty
sick; not bad for 80p!

The Ingleton Area

The Ingleton Area, whilst predominantly a cavers' domain, provides
many excellent watering holes and is worth a visit.

THE HILL INN (Worth a Visit)
CHAPEL-LE-DALE
NR INGLETON
VIA CARNFORTH
LANCASHIRE LA6 3AR
Telephone: (0468) 41256

Mine Host is Alan Greenbank. The pub is situated about 4½ miles from Ingleton on the B6255 to Hawes.

BEER
The Hill Inn is a free house selling Theakstons.

FOOD
Both bar snacks and restaurant food are served between the hours of 11.00 a.m. and 3.00 p.m. and in the evening from 5.30 p.m. to 10.00 p.m. The menu ranges from sandwiches, pie and peas (more of which later) to kebabs. Vegetarians are catered for.

FACILITIES
These include a games room, a pool table, a juke box, a dart board and public telephone. Dogs, children and muddy boots are all OK. The pub is well used by outdoor folk, including walkers, climbers and cavers. Camping is available here for 75p a night, although fires are not permitted so there are no jolly ging-gang-goolies round the campfire.

The site is adjacent to the pub and has overnight accommodation for fourteen.

OPINION
The Hill Inn, might be more aptly titled the Hillbilly Inn. This is the pub featured in Syd Perous's caving film, *The Underground Eiger*, which was a well-controlled riot. The Hill Inn is worth a visit for the atmosphere. Have you seen the film *Deliverance*? Well it's something along those lines. The surroundings are as basic as might be expected in a traditional cavers' pub and the exterior is peeling and uninviting. In order to appreciate fully the awfulness of this place the only time to arrive here is on a cold, wet windy midweek evening. The full set can then be properly digested. Inside is usually a full fire surrounded by tables made from old doors, a bit of a makeshift job this. It's the kind of pub that specializes in 'tricks', such as nailing a 50p piece to the floor so the locals can piss themselves watching newcomers try to remove it. A large wheel on the wall provides 'amusement', as one game is to try to squeeze through the spokes, cavers are very good at this sort of thing so be warned if you are challenged.

On the food side I tried a good old traditional Yorkshire dish 'pie and peas'. I thought 80p was quite cheap so I've no one to blame but myself really. Oh well, we live and learn . . .

The juke box is geared towards Status Quo fans and if you're not, well, after six pints you can get into it . . . and although a small sign states three for 10p, it doesn't really mean it, it's 1 for 10p. Sucker! There are toilets of sorts.

THE MARTEN ARMS (Recommended)
THORNTON IN LONGSDALE
INGLETON
CARNFORTH
LANCASHIRE LA6 3PB
Telephone: (0468) 41281

BEER
The Marten Arms is a free house serving ten types of beer including Theakstons.

FOOD
Bar snacks are served during licensing hours.

OPINION
This is now the 'in' pub for cavers in the Ingleton area and as such offers a good sporting Saturday night out. Mind you, cavers are such whimsical creatures, who knows where these shy bearded gentle folk will open their wallets next? At the moment this pub is definitely worth a visit. The beer is consistently good, according to one drunk I met there, and the food is good value. Music plays loudly and the atmosphere is one of good-natured jollity. Congenial landlord . . .

THE NEW INN
YEALAND CONYERS
NR CARNFORTH
LANCASHIRE
Telephone: (0524) 732938

Mine Hostess is Mrs Bernadine Taylor.

BEER
Hartleys.

FOOD
Bar snacks are served from 12.00 to about 2.00 p.m. with nothing for veggies.

FACILITIES
There is a games room, pool table, juke box, fruit machine and public telephone. Dogs are not allowed in, but children are. Muddy boots

should be removed before entering. There is camping at Silverdale 2–3 miles away.

COMMENT

There are two rooms, one without a bar. In busy periods climbers and walkers tend to congregate in one of these. Recommended in a good beer guide.

'Highly recommended' by Lancaster M.C. and Fylde M.C. after, before, or instead of a visit to Trowbarrow crag.

THE ROYAL ARMS
TOCKHOLES ROAD
DARWEN
LANCASHIRE BB3 0PU
Telephone: Darwen 75373

Mine Hosts are Arthur and Sylvia Jones. The pub is found by turning right approximately 2 miles north of Belmont on the Bolton/Preston road, the A675. It is signposted to Tockholes and the Royal is the first pub on the right.

BEER

The Royal is tied to the Thwaites Brewery.

FOOD

Both bar snacks and restaurant food are served between 12.00 and 2.00 p.m. and from 8.00 p.m. to 10.00 p.m., or at 7.00 p.m. by previous arrangement. There are no meals on Tuesday evenings. Veggies are OK here. Apart from a range of bar snacks, the menu offers a seafood platter with fresh lobster at £18 per head, all varieties of wild game, or rump steak cooked over an open fire . . . mmmmmm.

FACILITIES

There is a juke box. A public telephone is just outside the door of the pub. Dogs, children and muddy boots are OK.

THE SPORTSMANS ARMS (Recommended)
KEBCOTE
TODMORDEN
LANCASHIRE OL14 8SD
Telephone: Todmorden 3449

Mine Hostess is Mrs Jean Greenwood. The pub is found by travelling from Todmorden village via Cross Stove road/Eastwood road.

BEER
The pub is a free house.

FOOD
Both bar snacks and restaurant food are served. The serving times are from 12.00 to 3.00 p.m. and from 7.00 p.m. to 12.00 p.m. Vegetarian dishes are served. The menu varies from sandwiches to T-bone steaks. Reasonably priced.

FACILITIES
These include a games room, pool table, juke box and dart board. Dogs, children and muddy boots are OK here. Large open fires during the winter. Accommodation is available. There is room at the inn and camping available.
A good pub, popular with climbers and walkers. A separate room is available.

SWAN AND ROYAL HOTEL
CASTLE STREET
CLITHEROE
LANCASHIRE BB7 2BX
Telephone: (0200) 23130

Mine Hosts are Joseph and Julie Gallagher. The pub is found by turning off the A59 near Pendle Hill, and that road takes you into Clitheroe. The hotel is on the main road.

BEER
The pub is a free house.

FOOD
Bar snacks and restaurant food are available from 10.30 a.m. to 3.00 p.m. at dinnertime and from 7.00 p.m. to 11.00 p.m. in the evening. Vegetarians can breathe a sigh of relief. The menu ranges up to roast chicken at £3.25.

FACILITIES
There is a public telephone. Dogs and children are OK here. No muddy boots. B&B also.

THE WHITE HOUSE INN
BLACKSTONE EDGE
HALIFAX ROAD
LITTLEBOROUGH
LANCASHIRE
Telephone: (0706) 78456

The pub is found on the A58 between Littleborough and Ripponden (nr Halifax).

BEER
The White House is a free house.

FOOD
Bar snacks and restaurant food are available between the hours of 11.30 a.m. and 2.00 p.m. at dinnertime and between 7.00 p.m. and 10.00 p.m. in the evening. Vegetarians are catered for. The menu ranges from soup at 80p to sirloin steak at £4.25.

FACILITIES
These include a public telephone and no dogs, although children are allowed until 9.00 p.m. No muddy boots. There is camping on the nearby moors and the Pennine Way passes the door.

WILTON ARMS
BELMONT ROAD
BOLTON
LANCASHIRE
Telephone: (020453) 307

Mine Hosts are Mr and Mrs Bullock and the pub is very close to the Wilton Quarries.

BEER
This is a Whitbread pub.

FOOD
Bar snacks are served between 12.00 and 2.30 p.m., except Sundays when serving stops at 2.00 p.m. Evening food times are up to 9.30 p.m. approx on Mondays, Wednesdays, Thursdays and Saturdays. There's nothing done for the healthy eaters!

FACILITIES
These include a pool table, a juke box, a dart board and a public telephone. Dogs and children are acceptable if well behaved. Muddy boots are OK.

COMMENTS
'Used to be good, but alas! no more', and 'totally no good'.

Cafés

BERNI'S CAFÉ (Recommended)
INGLETON
LANCASHIRE

FOOD
The tea is a reasonable brew, a normal-size mug is 22p and a half-pint mug of coffee is 32p. The breakfast is good value at £1.60.

OPINION
This is the most popular and well-known café in the area, being the cavers' version of Stoney café or Pete's Eats. The café is said to be much improved since previous ownership and is now run by a caver who presumably knows the various needs and culinary desires of underground and outdoor folk and has endeavoured to satisy them. A mean lowly fire burns in the grate and the decor struggles to be basic. A few stalagmites and a bit of mud on the walls would make the clientele more comfortable. As it is caving surveys and pictures adorn the walls between the fruit machine and space invaders. A pool table is provided for sport.

The Lancashire Appendix

Pubs

THE BLACK BULL INN
WARTON

COMMENTS
'Mitchells beer OK.'

THE BOARS HEAD
HOGHTON
NR PRESTON

COMMENT
Handy for Hoghton Quarry, good restaurant facilities.

BOBS SMITHY INN
NR BROWNSTONES

Sited on the main Chorley old road.

COMMENTS
'Tetleys, very good. Not exactly a climbers' pub but good anyway.'

THE FLAG INN
EGERTON
NR BOLTON

COMMENT
Handy for Edgerton Quarry.

THE GOLDEN LION
MOORLANE
LANCASHIRE

Lancaster M.C. meet here on a Thursday from 9.30 p.m. onwards.

COMMENT
'The XB is particularly good.'

THE NAPIER INN
BOLTON ROAD
BURY
LANCASHIRE

Bury M.C. meet here on alternate Wednesdays from 8.30 p.m. onwards.

THE ROBIN HOOD
HELSBY
CHESHIRE

COMMENT
OK from Helsby, Frodsham or possibly Pex Hill.

THE THATCHED HOUSE
BALL STREET
POULTON LE FYLDE

The active types from the Fylde M.C. meet here on Wednesdays from 9.00 p.m. onwards. The Boddingtons is better than in the Breck Sports Club, the other meeting place of the club.

THE TRAVELLERS REST
HIGHLANDS ROAD
FROGSMOUTH QUARRY
NR RUNCORN

COMMENT
Handy for Frogsmouth Quarry.

THE YEW TREE
HORWICH
NR BOLTON
LANCASHIRE

COMMENT
OK for Anglezarke Quarry.

Other Venues

THE BRECK SPORTS CLUB
72 BRECK ROAD
POULTON LE FYLDE

A venue for slide shows and meeting place of the Fylde M.C., also on Wednesdays from 9.00 p.m. onwards. Do I detect a split in the ranks?

The North York Moors

———◆———

'Breathless, we flung us on the windy hill
Laughed in the sun, and kissed the lovely grass'

RUPERT BROOKE

There are very few active climbers in the area, in fact there are only two, and they've both left so the hard rock scene is fairly low key. Good! This just means that there is more peace and quiet for those of us who visit.

It is very pretty and surprise! surprise! another National Park. How fortunate that crags are not indigenous to grotty places, Stoney Middleton and Dumbarton Rock excepted. We climbers are very lucky in that our chosen sport takes us to such ace places, how absolutely sick-making if one was caught up with inner city decay and urban hopelessness. But it doesn't so on with the discourse.

The scene, if it exists at all, must be mellow since the four climbers I met were laid back. It was in a pub and they claimed to be rockers and had I been to Donnington?

On Sunday afternoons you are quite likely to meet like minded souls at the more popular edges, although they tend to be the type who wear helmets with their names on and refuse to use their knees. Here you can be a star!

The Climbing

The consistent factor about North York climbing is the height of the crags, or rather lack of it. All the crags involve a brisk walk over moorland and peat, to be

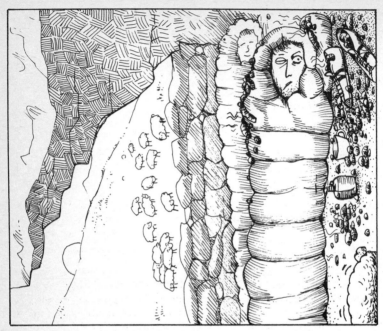

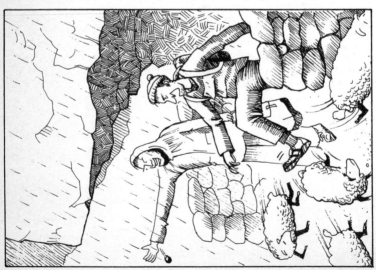

Sleeping rough

welcomed by some reassuringly small crags (sometimes called 'craglets'), and a comfortingly large selection of low grade classics to float around on.

Pubs

THE JET MINERS INN (Worth a Visit)
HIGH STREET
GT BROUGHTON
STOKESLEY
MIDDLESBROUGH
CLEVELAND TS9 7HB
Telephone: (0642) 712427

Mine Host is Mr Patrick Willis and the pub is found by travelling from Stokesley on the Helmsley Road (B1257) for about 2 miles.

BEER
The pub is a free house serving two traditional ales and lager.

FOOD
Bar snacks and restaurant food are served. The menu is on a blackboard which changes regularly, varying from homemade beefburger and chips at £1.20, to steak and ale pie at £3.85. Serving times are up to 2.00 p.m. at dinnertime and between 6.30 p.m. and 10.00 p.m. in the evening.

FACILITIES
These are a games room, pool table, juke box, dart board and public telephone. Dogs are allowed at the landlord's discretion and children are OK, but no muddy boots. There is a camping and caravan site with toilet and showers. It is close to the North York Moors, the Cleveland Way and the Lyke Wake walk and is mentioned in other guides.

OPINION
The pub is popular with climbers in the area, although they are a bit thin on the ground.

SUTTON ARMS
FACEBY
NR STOKESLEY
MIDDLESBROUGH PS9 7BW
Telephone: (0642) 700382

Mine Host is Mr Teasdale and the pub is found by turning right off the A172 towards Stokesley, into Faceby village.

BEER
Tied to Camerons.

FOOD
Only snacks are served, such as toasties, pie and peas, and other basic dishes.

FACILITIES
There is a pool table, a juke box and dart board. A public telephone is just outside the pub. No dogs. Children are OK for Sunday dinner (lightly toasted please) and in the early evening. There is camping 2 miles away at Carlton-in-Cleveland.

COMMENT
'Quite good, worth a visit.'

WAINSTONES INN
GT BROUGHTON
MIDDLESBROUGH
CLEVELAND PS9 7EW
Telephone: (0642) 712268

Mine Host is Mr Stephens.

BEER
This is a free house (see below).

FOOD
Both bar snacks and restaurant food are served. Times are from 12.00 to 2.00 p.m., with the restaurant finishing at 1.30 p.m. In the evening, times are from 7.00 p.m. to 10.00 p.m. These times apply every day of the year except Christmas because 'we need at least one day off a year'. (It's no wonder this country is going to the dogs!)

FACILITIES
There is a games room with a pool table for residents. A public phone in the pub. No dogs but kids OK. Boots within reason are OK. There are camp sites within 3–4 miles. Accommodation is available at the inn and if you stop over, the management sometimes gives you a lift to the top of Clay Bank Hill! How's that for service!

COMMENT
Reasonably well used by climbers and walkers. Recommended in CAMRA (two real ales are served) and Les Routiers.
   'Good.'

Cafés

WELCOME CAFÉ (OK)
THORNTON LE DALE
PICKERING
YORKSHIRE
Telephone: (0751) 74272

Proprietors are R. W. and G. Baldersons.

OPENING TIMES
The café is open seven days a week from 9.30 a.m. to 5.45 p.m.

OPINION
OK, although tending to attract the elderly coach party trade. There is seating for 120 so there will usually be room. Prices are above Basic Caff level, but the goodies on offer are worth it. Everything has fresh cream in it. Scrumptious!

Tourist Information in the North York Moors National Park

The centres are at:

Danby, *Tel: Castleton (0287) 60654*
Helmsley, *Tel: Helmsley (0439) 70657*
Hutton Le Hole, *Tel: Lastingham (07515) 367*
Middlesbrough, *Tel: Middlesbrough (0642) 245432*
Pickering, *Tel: Pickering (0751) 73791*
Scarborough, *Tel: Scarborough (0723) 373333*
Sutton Bank, *Tel: Thirsk (0845) 597426*
Thirsk, *Tel: Thirsk (0845) 22755*
Whitby, *Tel: Whitby (0947) 602674*
York, *Tel: York (0904) 21756/7*

The North Yorks Appendix

CLAY BANK CAR PARK SNACK BAR

This is the parking area for climbing at Hasty Bank and a small shack serves tea and beefburgers.

The Lake District

————

"Ah don't say you agree with me. When people agree with me I always feel that I must be wrong.'

OSCAR WILDE

The Lake District – the Lakes – reminds me of Wythen-shawe public baths on a Saturday afternoon; wet and busy. Either condition should be enough to discourage most visitors, but no, the Lake District is a popular holiday venue for visitors from all over Britain. At first glance the area might seem to be composed entirely of caravans, speed boats and traffic jams. This view is misleading. The area also contains screaming kids, fat Americans and Ye Olde Tea Shoppes.

In fact, the Lake District has something to annoy everyone, a multi-functional National Park combining all the elements of a really rotten day out; heavy traffic, overcrowded towns, overpriced coffee shops and lousy weather. So what is the attraction? Well, unless you are half blind (like most of the drivers up there), one sunny afternoon spent drifting across Grasmere Lake, or rambling over Great Gable will be enough to win your heart for ever. It is a particularly beautiful place.

Wordsworth expressed his love for the area on many occasions. His love of nature is well known and his better known musings are oft spake – lonely daffodil wanderings and so on – but I prefer a less well worn and rarely quoted line, one uttered as he gazed from his study window, the autumn leaves turning golden brown and

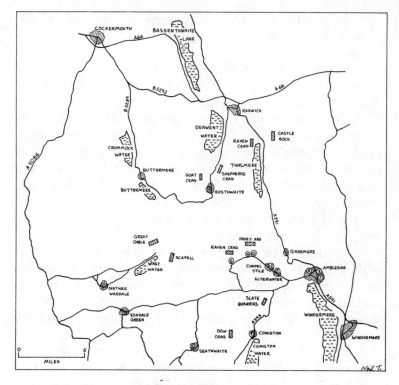

THE LAKE DISTRICT

PUBS

1 **THE BOWER HOUSE INN**
Eskdale Green
2 **THE BRITANNIA INN**
Elterwater
3 **THE GOLDEN RULE**
Ambleside
4 **THE NEW DUNGEON GHYLL
HOTEL** Gt Langdale
5 **NEWFIELD INN** Seathwaite
6 **THE OLD DUNGEON
GHYLL** Gt Langdale

7 **THE SALUTATION INN**
Ambleside
8 **SCAFELL HOTEL** Rosthwaite
9 **THE SHIP INN** Coniston
10 **STICKLEBARN TAVERN**
Gt Langdale
11 **THE STRANDS HOTEL**
Nether Wasdale
12 **WAINWRIGHTS INN**
Chapel Stile

CAFÉ

A **STOCK GHYLL CAFÉ** Ambleside

fluttering in the breeze, clouds gathering ominously: 'Oh bloody hell, it's raining again and I've just put me washing out'.

That simple line, wrung from the heart, captures the spirit of the Lake District for me – 'it's raining again'. Aah! Such eloquence and how true!

Apart from the weather, the layout of the lakes leaves much to be desired. There are only two or three well-positioned crags, Scout Crag, Raven Crag and the Bowderstone which might be a boulder to local climbers, but is a good-sized crag by Peak standards. The other crags are miles away, taking several days to reach by mule, or a couple of hours to walk. Either way, they are a long long slog. Small wonder that no one, except loonies and Chris Bonington, climbs on the mountain cliffs. Chris says that walking up to the high crags strengthens his leg muscles for keeping up with the Sherpas on Himalayan trips. Sherpas are noted for their strength and endurance and, apart from Chris's computer bearer, they can move pretty quickly.

To be fair to the place, the Lake District is quite magnificent – you can see that for yourself – it's just that it's a bit ... well ... organized. Well managed and crowded. Some people prefer it like that, but I like my wilderness undiluted and next time I shall definitely avoid bank holiday weekends because if one more busybody tells me, 'That dog should be on a lead. Can't you read the signs?', I shall say something unpleasant. How strange that people feel compelled to obey orders because they are displayed on boards: read the small print on the back of the by-laws which states that dogs should be 'kept under control' with no mention of leads. It's interesting to note that all the farmers I meet chat pleasantly, saying, 'Eeh, bye 'eck, that's a grand little dog. Ah wouldn't mind a pup off 'er'. During the conversation Bill is usually cowering and baring her teeth. Farmers like dogs like that.

One redeeming feature of the area is the pubs. Many are traditional, heaving with outdoor folk after an exhausting day's adventures. The Lake District is not as popular with hard climbers as it once was; the pickings are more easily accessible down south, consequently there are no Prima Donnas and everyone climbs for 'the right reasons', whatever they are.

Pubs

THE BOWER HOUSE INN
ESKDALE GREEN
HOLMROOK
CUMBRIA CA19 1TD
Telephone: (09403) 244

The Bower House is a free house and is found by travelling northbound along the A595 and turning left at either Gosforth or Holmrook.

FOOD
Bar snacks and restaurant food are served between 12.00 and 2.00 p.m. and from 6.30 p.m. to 9.00 p.m. Also vegetarian dishes.

FACILITIES
These include a public telephone and drying room. Overnight accommodation. Also mentioned in good food/beer guides and popular with climbers and walkers.

COMMENTS
Highly recommended.

THE BRITANNIA INN
ELTERWATER
AMBLESIDE
CUMBRIA LA22 9HP
Telephone: (09667) 210 or 382

Mine Host is David Fry and the pub is found by following the A593 Ambleside to Conniston road. Fork right 2½ miles from Ambleside, at Skelwith bridge, onto the B5343. After 1¼ miles, it comes into Elterwater village.

BEER
The pub is a free house.

FOOD

Bar snacks are served from 12.00 to 2.00 p.m. and between 6.30 p.m. and 9.00 p.m. Restaurant food is served from 7.30 p.m. onwards. Vegetarian dishes are served. The food varies from baps at 90p, bar meals up to £4 and dinner up to £13. There is an extensive food and drink takeaway service about which more information can be found at the bar.

FACILITIES

There is a dart board, a public telephone and dogs and children are welcome, although muddy boots are frowned upon. Accommodation is available, a single room costing from £18 in the high season and from £14 in the low season.

COMMENT

Recommended in various guides, RAC, AA, Egon Ronay, BTA, English Tourist Guide (2 crowns) and good food and beer guides.
   'Worth a visit.'

THE GOLDEN RULE (Recommended)
SMITHY BROW
AMBLESIDE
CUMBRIA LA22
Telephone: (09 66) 33363/32257

Mine Hosts are John Christopher Lockley and Margaret Elizabeth Lockley. The Rule is found by turning right at the Kirkstone Pass sign when leaving Ambleside on the Rydal road. The pub is instantly visible from the bottom of the hill.

BEER

The pub is tied to Hartleys Brewery.

FOOD

Bar snacks are served at lunchtime.

FACILITIES

These include a games room with a dart board. There is a public telephone. Dogs, children and muddy boots are allowed in.

OPINION

Definitely the place for climbers and walkers in the area. Very congenial atmosphere and useful for meeting local climbers. When asked if there was a separate room for climbers, such as a Hikers Bar, the reply was that all four rooms were for climbers. A succinct answer.

THE NEW DUNGEON GHYLL HOTEL
GREAT LANGDALE
AMBLESIDE
CUMBRIA
Telephone: (09667) 213

Mine Host is Sean Hopkins. The pub is at the bottom of Sickle Ghyll in Great Langdale. This is on the A593 out of Ambleside.

BEER
The New D.G. is a free house.

FOOD
Bar snacks are served between 11.00 a.m. and 3.00 p.m. and also from 5.30 p.m. to 11.00 p.m. Can't say fairer than that. Vegetarians are shunned. Ha, ha.

FACILITIES
There is a dart board and a public telephone. Dogs, muddy children and boots are acceptable. Bunkhouse accommodation is next door and the camp site is half a mile away.

OPINION
You could be forgiven for expecting the New D.G. to be a more modern version of the Old D.G. You'd be wrong. It is even more basic! It is well patronized by walkers and climbers and has its own peculiar charm. Sitting outside is recommended.

NEWFIELD INN
SEATHWAITE
BROUGHTON IN FURNESS
CUMBRIA LA20 6ED
Telephone: (06576) 208

Mine Host is John Stuart Batten and the pub is found by travelling 1 mile north of Broughton on the A595 then turn right and go 6 miles up the valley, from Langdale over Wrynose Pass to Cockley Beck then 4 miles down the valley.

BEER
The pub is a free house.

FOOD
Both bar snacks and restaurant food are available during the hours of 12.00 to 2.30 p.m. and 6.00 p.m. to 9.00 p.m. except Sundays when the hours are 12.00 to 1.45 p.m. and 7.00 p.m. to 9.00 p.m. Vegetarian palates are titivated.

FACILITIES
There is a pool table and public telephone. Dogs are allowed on a lead.
Muddy boots are OK. Children under supervision are OK up to
8.00 p.m. There is a good cheap camp site a quarter of a mile up the
road, and also two self catering flats attached to the pub.

OPINION
The pub is used by many climbers and is recommended in other
guides.

THE OLD DUNGEON GHYLL (Recommended)
GREAT LANGDALE
AMBLESIDE
CUMBRIA LA22 9JY
Telephone: (09667) 272

Mine Host is Neil Walmsley. The Old D.G. is found by travelling from
Ambleside along the A593 to the head of Great Langdale. The pub is at
the foot of Langdale Pikes.

BEER
The pub is a free house selling Theakstons and Youngers ales.

FOOD
Both bar snacks and restaurant food are available. Advance booking is
advisable for the sit-down job. Serving times are between 12.00 and
2.00 p.m. and from 6.00 p.m. to 8.00 p.m. They take pity on vegetarians.
The menu ranges from sandwiches to scampi.

FACILITIES
A dart board and public telephone. Dogs, children and muddy boots
allowed. The Old D.G. has fourteen letting bedrooms, climbing and
walking clubs are welcomed and there is a National Trust camp site
within five minutes' walk.

OPINION
The pub has a reputation amongst the outdoor fraternity for tradition
and atmosphere. It certainly feels old. Worth a visit for the atmosphere.
Reminiscent of one's drunken student days, if that's a good thing.

THE SALUTATION INN (known as the Sally Inn)
LAKE ROAD
AMBLESIDE
CUMBRIA LA22 9BX
Telephone: Ambleside 32244

Mine Host is Geoffrey Atkinson. The pub is located in the centre of the village at the beginning of Stock Ghyll walk, on the main A592 road.

BEER
The Sally is a free house.

FOOD
Both bar snacks and restaurant food are served between 12.00 and 2.30 p.m. and between 6.00 p.m. to 9.30 p.m. Vegetarians are catered for on request.

FACILITIES
There is a games room, pool table, a juke box, dart board and a public telephone. Dogs, children and muddy boots are OK here.

OPINION
The Sally has had a long association with climbers, although it is no longer 'the' watering hole in Ambleside. However, the pub is the recognized meeting point for Stock Ghyll and Fairfield walks as mentioned in various guidebooks. There is a large car park and easy access from the main road. On the accommodation side B&B is reduced from £15 to £12.50 for climbing club members.

A large and busy pub.

THE SHIP INN
CONISTON
CUMBRIA LA21 8HB
Telephone: (0966) 41224

Mine Hosts are Derrick and Linda Freedman. The pub is found by following the A593 through Coniston towards Torver, approximately ½ mile from the village of Coniston.

BEER
The Ship is tied to Hartleys of Ulverston Ltd.

FOOD
Superior bar snacks are offered. Dinner is served from 12.00 to 2.00 p.m. and teatime from 5.30 p.m. to 9.30 p.m. Vegetarian meals are available on request. The menu varies from soup at 80p to sirloin steak at £5.25. There is also a children's menu.

FACILITIES
There is a games room, pool table, juke box and dart board. Dogs, children and muddy boots are OK. This is the nearest pub to the local camp site and caravan site.

OPINION
Much used by climbers and walkers.

STICKLEBARN TAVERN (Recommended)
NEW DUNGEON GHYLL
GT LANGDALE
NR AMBLESIDE LA22 9JY
Telephone: (09667) 356

Mine Hosts are Graham and Kataleen Hill. The pub is found by
following the signs from Ambleside to Coniston and Langdale. Bear
right at Skelwith Bridge on the B5343 and continue to Chapel Stile and
Great Langdale. The Sticklebarn is 2½ miles further on, on the right.

BEER
The pub is a free house.

FOOD
Bar snacks and restaurant food are served from 8.30 a.m. to 10.30 p.m.
all day! Vegetarian food is served. Food ranges from soup at 95p to
sirloin steak at £5.95.

FACILITIES
There is a games room, a pool table, juke box, dart board and public
telephone. There is also bunkhouse accommodation at £5.75 a night
with group discounts available. No dogs, children or muddy boots
allowed. Recommended in food and beer guides.

THE STRANDS HOTEL
NETHER WASDALE
NR GOSFORTH
CUMBRIA CA20 1ET
Telephone: 237

Mine Host is Mr A. Benton and the pub is found by turning left off the
A595 to Workington at the Gosforth Junction and following the Nether
Wasdale signs.

BEER
The Strands is a free house.

FOOD
Both bar snacks and restaurant food are served. Vegetarians are catered
for.

FACILITIES
There is a games room, dart board and public telephone. Can cater for
small parties and supply campers' breakfasts. Dogs, children and muddy
boots are all allowed in the games room. There is a separate bar for
climbers and walkers and the pub is recommended in a food and beer
guide.

THE THREE SHIRES INN
LITTLE LANGDALE
AMBLESIDE
CUMBRIA
Telephone: (09667) 215

Mine Hosts are the Stephenson family and the pub is sited at the eastern foot of Wrynose Pass.

BEER
The Three Shires is a free house.

FOOD
Both bar meals and restaurant food are served from 12.00 to 2.00 p.m. and from 6.30 p.m. to 9.00 p.m. Prices vary from £1.00 to £9.00 for bar meals and from £11.25 in the restaurant.

FACILITIES
There is a dart board and a public telephone. Dogs are allowed in the bar only and children are OK to roam freely. Muddy boots are allowed in the bar which has a green slate floor. There are several 'high quality' bedrooms.

COMMENTS
Comments vary from 'absolutely rubbish' to highly recommended, 'good value bar meals'. It is well used by outdoor folk. When asked if the pub was recommended in other guides, the comment was 'yes, most'. So there.

WAINWRIGHTS INN
CHAPEL STILE
GT LANGDALE
CUMBRIA LA23 9JF
Telephone: (09667) 253

Mine Hostess is Mrs Quine.

BEER
A free house.

FOOD
Bar snacks are available between 12.00 and 1.45 p.m. and from 7.00 p.m. to 9.15 p.m. Veggie types can breath again.

FACILITIES
Piped music (aah!), a dart board and public phone are all offered for your delight. Dogs, kids and boots are OK. There is camping and B&B within walking distance.

COMMENT
The pub is well used by climbers and walkers and is 'worth a visit'.

Café

STOCK GHYLL CAFÉ
AMBLESIDE
CUMBRIA
Telephone: (05394) 33334

This is the café opposite Frank Davies's shop and up a bit.

FOOD
A full breakfast is available up till 11.30 a.m. and costs £2.15. A small tea is 23p and a large one is 25p.

OPINION
The decor is à la formica with artificial wood panelling tastelessly mixed with Lakeland rock of slate and granite. Not that it matters. The only gripe is the lack of toilet facilities. The nearest are in the main car park. Apologies were given but that wasn't what I required.

One feature is the presence of the local police force who practise 'lurking' in the kitchens . . . community policing just boils down to drinking tea and lurking.

Lake District Tourist Information

These are:

Brockhole National Park, Tel: (09662) 6601
Whinlatter, Tel: (059682) 469
Blencathra, Tel: (059683) 601

Visitor Information Centres

Alston, Tel: (0498) 81696
Ambleside, Tel: (0966) 32582
Appleby, Tel: (0930) 51177
Bowness, Tel: (09662) 5602
Bownes Bay, Tel: (09662) 2895
Brampton, Tel: (06977) 3433
Carlisle, Tel: (0228) 25517
Grange over sands, Tel: (04484) 4026
Grasmere, Tel: (09665) 245
Hawkshead, Tel: (09666) 525
Kendal, Tel: (0539) 25758

Keswick, Tel: (0596) 72803
Kirby Stephen, Tel: (0930) 71603
Penrith, Tel: (0768) 67466
Pooley Bridge, Tel: (08536) 530
Seatoller, Tel: (059684) 294
Sedbergh, Tel: (0587) 20125
Southwaite M6 motorway, Tel: (06993) 445
Ullswater (Glenridding), Tel: (08532) 414
Ulverston, Tel: (0229) 57120
Waterhead (Ambleside), Tel: (0966) 32729
Windermere, Tel: (09662) 6499

Felltop Weather Forecast

Tel: (09662) 5151

National Park Ranger Service

Tel: (09662) 6601

The Lake District Appendix

THE GEORGE HOTEL
PETTERDALE
CUMBRIA

COMMENT
'Worth a visit.'

THE SCAFELL HOTEL
BORROWDALE
NR KESWICK
CUMBRIA
Telephone: (059684) 208

OPINION
There is a separate climbers' bar around the back which is very basic but functional. There is also a 'patio' for overlooking the stream and enjoying the warm summer evening, or, if it's cold, casting dagger glances at those inside who managed to get seats. A popular drinking hole with outdoor folk.

HOLLIES 24-HOUR CAFÉ (for travellers Lake District bound)

COMMENT
Turn off the M6 north of Birmingham, signposted A5, towards Cannock. 'Don't go between 2.00 a.m. and 7.00 a.m. unless absolutely desperate.'

Northumberland

There is a land far away where solitude reigns supreme, where the hills roll in every direction, where the rock is sound and the crags are small, where the beaches stretch over the horizon, where you can spend days and never spot a pair of lycra dance tights.

Northumberland must be one of the last strongholds of Mother Nature in Britain, tucked away in the north east, rarely visited and quite unspoilt; it is a place of perfections. However, as with any earthly paradise, there are faults and here the problem – a mere problemette – is that it is an awfully long way away. Doubtless the reason for retaining the area's magical qualities, but popping up for a weekend's cragging requires patience and perseverance; the A1 seems to go for ever. But it is worth it and you can pass the time by playing various car games, such as hitting the brakes sharply in front of learner drivers or flicking Vs and mooning at coach loads of football supporters.

The Climbing

Bowden Doors
Having negotiated the haul up there, you will turn your attention to the crags. The best well known must be

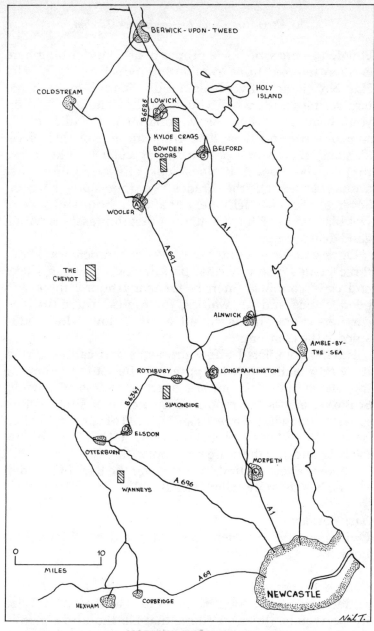

NORTHUMBERLAND

PUBS
1 **BIRD IN BUSH INN** Elsdon
2 **THE BLACK BULL** Lowick
3 **THE BLACK SWAN** Belford

4 **JOINERS ARMS** Morpeth
5 **LINDEN PUB** Long Framlington
6 **TANNERS ARMS** Alnwick
7 **THE WHITE SWAN** Lowick

CAFÉ A **THE RENDEZVOUS CAFÉ** Wooler

Bowden Doors which is a proper treat. The climbing here is often referred to as 'bouldering' which is a joke. Ha! Ha! No chance! I've been around and I know what bouldering is. It's when you can fall off the top, land on your head and walk away unharmed. I'd like to see someone try and nose dive from the top of this place. (Actually there's one person in particular I'd like to see try.) To be honest it does look fairly short on first acquaintance and the grades are innocuous enough; Severes, VSs and such like, but after an hour and several wobbles, you will have to temper first impressions with a good deal of respect.

Once you have found your level of competence, about three grades below normal performance, you can shake and claw your way merrily for many hours; there is a good choice and no waiting for routes. There are few climbers. Some holds sound a bit hollow which adds spice to the climbing.

Having completed a few problems and earned a rest, it's worth taking time to appreciate the setting. From the top of the crag you can see beaches and small islands. Scattered across the moorlands, patches of sunlit cotton grass dance in light breezes and the call of curlews is often heard. The views are magnificent, a titillation of the eyeballs and still there are no people.

There is another climbing area over the back of Bowden Doors. It is sensibly called Back Bowden.

Back Bowden
Quite good but nowhere near the standard of its neighbour.

Kyloe in the Woods
Hidden amongst a lot of trees there is a crag called Kyloe in the Woods. (It seems to me that Northumbrians go in for sensible crag names.) What a lovely name it is though

– Kyloe in the Woods! It is worth a visit on the strength of that alone. And the situation is just charming. To reach the climbing you walk through an increasingly dense wood and it gets quieter and quieter and a bit spooky. The odd shaft of sunlight penetrates, highlighting ferns and mosses – an enchanted forest, reminiscent of the Gnomemobile film. I half expected to meet the little people and the fairies.

Sorry to say that, having arrived, the pleasure soon dissipates. It is one of those places described as 'an esoteric gem' which means it is too hard. The climbing is mainly bouldering, since it is impossible to get high enough to hurt yourself. Fortunately the landings are excellent, soft and bouncy, but boot cleaning loses its appeal after the hundredth time. Names like Bob Smith and Pete Kirton start to assume god-like qualities.

Pubs

BIRD IN BUSH INN
ELSDON
NR OTTERBURN
NORTHUMBERLAND NE19 1AA
Telephone: (0830) 20478

Mine Host is Mr Arthur Furnival. The pub is found by turning off 2½ miles before Otterburn on the A696.

FOOD
A restaurant is open between the hours of 12.00 and 2.00 p.m. and from 7.00 p.m. to 9.00 p.m. Vegetarians are tolerated.

FACILITIES
There is a dart board. Dogs, children and muddy boots are acceptable. The pub borders the Northumberland National Park. The pub is 350 years old and is a listed building.

OPINION
Handy for Sandy Crag and South Yardhope. As a pub it's 'OK'.

THE BLACK BULL
MAIN STREET
LOWICK
BERWICK UPON TWEED
NORTHUMBERLAND TD15 2UN
Telephone: (028988) 228

Mine Hosts are Anne and Tom Grundy.

BEER
The Bull is a free house and is about 5 miles off the A1 through
Fenwick.

FOOD
Bar snacks are served and there may soon be a new restaurant opening.
Food is served during pub opening times with last food orders being
taken 1½ hours before closing time. Food isn't available on Mondays
during the winter.

FACILITIES
These include a pool table (in the smallest room possible), a juke box
and a dart board. Dogs are not allowed and children are only allowed
up to 8.30 p.m. if eating. Muddy boots are usually left at the door.
There is a self-catering cottage next to the pub and there are camp sites
at Ford 4–5 miles away or at Berwick Upon Tweed. There is supposed
to be a caravan site opening in the village soon, yuk!

OPINION
A reasonably pleasant pub tending to get busy with people eating.
They are recommended in the *Good Beer Guide* and CAMRA.

THE BLACK SWAN (Recommended)
MARKET PLACE
BELFORD
NORTHUMBERLAND NE70 7ND
Telephone: (06683) 266

Mine Host is Mr Stevenson.

BEER
The Swan is a free house and is found by leaving the A1 at Belford, into
the village and there it is!

FOOD
Bar snacks and breakfast are served between 12.00 and 2.00 p.m. and
from 7.00 p.m. to 8.30 p.m. every day except Wednesdays when you'll
have to find a chippy. Vegetarian dishes are served.

FACILITIES
There is a games room, pool table, juke box and three dart boards!!
Crikey that's one each! There are also video game machines and 'triv'
is also played! Dogs are allowed on leads as are kids and muddy boots.
B&B is available at the pub from £11.50, otherwise there is a camp site
nearby.

OPINION
Another jolly pub, recommended in the AA guide. Helpful landlord.

JOINERS ARMS
7 WANSBECK STREET
MORPETH
NORTHUMBERLAND NE61 1X2
Telephone: (0670) 513540

Mine Host is Bob Jackson and the pub is off Castle Square before
crossing the River Wansbeck.

BEER
A free house (see below).

FOOD
No food is served.

FACILITIES
Dogs are allowed in and children are not (quite right too). Muddy
boots are OK.

COMMENT
Mine Host says, and I quote, 'This is probably one of the few
remaining bars where the only entertainment is your own conversation. No telly, no piped music or juke box. We also offer a selection of
three traditional ales and keg and tank beer. This is a small town pub,
not really on a walker's route but very close to the beautiful North-
umbrian countryside.' In the *Good Beer Guide*.
   OK for a stop-off from Corbys Crag.

LINDEN PUB
LINDEN HALL HOTEL
LONG FRAMLINGTON/LONG HORSLEY
MORPETH
NORTHUMBERLAND NE65 8XG
Telephone: (0670) 516611 ext 279

The Linden is a free house and is off the A697 road between Long Horsley and Long Framlington, down the main hotel drive and situated behind the hotel.

FOOD
Bar meals are served including vegetarian food. Times for food are 12.00 to 2.30 p.m. and 6.30 p.m. to 9.00 p.m. from Monday to Saturday. Sunday serving times are 12.00 to 2.00 p.m. and from 7.00 p.m. to 9.00 p.m.

FACILITIES
There is a pool table, dart board and public telephone. Guide dogs only are allowed and children have to go upstairs. Dry muddy boots are allowed. There is overnight accommodation at the main hotel.

OPINION
They are recommended in the *Good Pub Guide*. Not many climbers or walkers use the pub.

TANNERS ARMS (Highly Recommended)
HOTSPUR PLACE
ALNWICK
NORTHUMBERLAND NE66 1QF
Telephone: (0665) 602553

Mine Hosts are Winston and Ann Hardishy and the pub is found by taking the A1 into Alnwick and turning left before the archway into town. The Tanners is 200 yards up the hill on the left corner.

BEER
A free house (see below).

FOOD
Sandwiches only are served at the following times: Sundays 12.00 to 2.00 p.m. and 7.00 p.m. to 10.30 p.m. Wednesdays, Thursdays, Fridays and Saturdays between 12.00 and 3.00 p.m. and from 7.00 p.m. to 10.30 p.m. with an extra half an hour serving Friday and Saturday evenings. From May to the end of September, closing is 11.00 p.m. No rabbit food.

FACILITIES
There is a juke box, dogs are OK, but children are only allowed in at dinnertimes. Muddy boots are all right within reason.

OPINION
Mine Host said, 'Our main sales are Real Ale, we do not sell keg beers, just this; we concentrate just on the ale. This is why we do not cater.'

Excellent!! This is the right attitude for a landlord! The pub is recommended in the *Good Beer Guide*. Highly recommended.

THE WHITE SWAN (Worth a Visit)
LOWICK
BERWICK UPON TWEED
NORTHUMBERLAND
Telephone: (0289 88) 249

Mine Host is Roy Cossar.

BEER
Beer sold is Stones and Newcastle.

FOOD
Bar snacks and a dining room are available from 12.00 to 2.00 p.m. During the evening dining is usually bookable.

FACILITIES
There is a games room, pool table, juke box and dart board. The nearest public phone is 20 yards away. Dogs on leads are allowed in and children are OK. Muddy boots are OK. There are two B&Bs in the village or, if you're really stuck, camping can be arranged in the landlord's field.

OPINION
A grand little pub this. The sort of place where breakaway groups are not permitted; there is one big conversation taking place and everyone contributes. It's very friendly. A locals' pub with civilized hospitality.

Cafés

THE RENDEZVOUS CAFÉ
6 PETH HEAD
WOOLER
NORTHUMBERLAND
Telephone: (066881) 227

OPENING HOURS
These are from 7.00 a.m. to 10.00 p.m. all week except Sundays when times are 9.00 a.m. to 8.00 p.m.

OPINION
A good basic caff serving reasonable value food and drink in clean surroundings. Friendly service.

The Northumberland Appendix

Pubs

THE BIRD
TANTOBIE
CO. DURHAM

COMMENT
'OK' handy for Causey Quarry.

BRANDLING VILLAS
SOUTH GOSFORTH
NEWCASTLE UPON TYNE

Northumbria M.C. meet here during the winter (October–March) on Wednesdays about 8.30 p.m.

DURHAM CITY RUGBY F.C.
GREEN LAND
DURHAM

Durham M.C. meet here on the first Monday of each month at 8.30 p.m.

THE ERRINGTON ARMS

Sited on the A65/B6318 crossroads north of Corbridge.

COMMENT
'OK.' Handy for Peel Crag and Crag Lough.

THE NEUK
MARKET PLACE
BEDLINGTON
NORTHUMBERLAND

Wanneys C.C. meet here on the first Wednesday of each month at 8.00 p.m.

THE RAILWAY HOTEL
ROTHBURY
NORTHUMBERLAND

COMMENT
'Worth a visit and handy from Simonside, Ravensheugh and Selbys Cove.'

Cafés

CHEVIOT CHARLIE'S CAFÉ
WOOLER
NORTHUMBERLAND

COMMENT
'Worth a visit.'

THE EAT AGAIN

5 miles south of Belford on the A1.

COMMENT
'Worth a visit.' Good food and beer.

Chip Shops

There are chip shops near to the pubs in the following towns: Bedlington, Morpeth, Alnwick and Rothbury, the latter being recommended.

North Wales

'I waved and went outside
And I headed for the mountains
Feeling warm inside
I love that Bedford van so much
You know that I could kiss her'

LOU REED (with adaptations by G. FAWCETT)

Over the last ten years I have grown to love North Wales. It has been a second home to me; cold, bleak and depressing. I spent three happy years as an undergraduate at Bangor University, relieving my childhood and glorying in the company of my fellow BUMS. What adventures we embarked on; our young, innocent fresh faces flushed with drink. It all comes flooding back now . . . midnight ascents of Lockwoods Chimney, barbecues by Llyn Gwynant, epic winter ascents on Craig Yrsfa and epic summer ascents at Tremadog. Come to think of it there were lots of epics but also lots of fun. Things were Traditional then, certain things were done because they'd always been done, and hopefully will continue.

The Victorian Tea Party by the side of Llyn Ogwen in February was one such occasion. Snow lay all around. Champagne and cucumber sandwiches, sans crusts, set the scene for the various misinterpretations of Victorian dress. For some reason, now lost in the mists of time, I went pregnant, a cushion up the frock did the trick. This paid dividends as I was courteously escorted over the stiles by Dr Marshall, a vice President and a sport if ever I

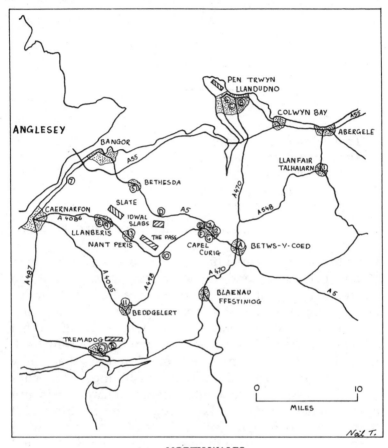

NORTH WALES

PUBS

1 **THE BLACK LION** Llanfair Talhaiarn
2 **BRYN TYRCH HOTEL** Capel Curig
3 **COBDENS HOTEL** Capel Curig
4 **COTTAGE LOAF** Llandudno
5 **THE DOUGLAS ARMS** Bethesda
6 **THE GOLDEN FLEECE** Tremadog
7 **HALFWAY HOUSE** Port Dinorwig
8 **THE KINGS HEAD** Llandudno

9 **THE PADARN LAKE HOTEL**
Llanberis
10 **PENYGWRYD HOTEL**
Nantgwynant
11 **SARACEN'S HEAD HOTEL**
Beddgelert
12 **TYN Y COED** Capel Curig
13 **THE VAYNOL ARMS** Nant Peris

CAFÉS

A **ANCASTER MILK BAR**
Betws-y-Coed
B **ERIC'S CAFÉ** Tremadog
C **HAPPY VALLEY CAFÉ** Llandudno
D **OGWEN FALLS SNACK BAR**
Ogwen Cottage

E **PETE'S EATS** Llanberis
F **THE PINNACLE CAFÉ** Capel Curig
G **THE SNOWDONIA CAFÉ**
Capel Curig

met one. My 'condition' proved useful for balancing the ashtray on. Oh, happy days . . .

But the name of North Wales conjures up a myriad images. The land of traffic jams and road works. The land where all paths lead to Llwybr Cyhoedous.

Aah, but enough jibes, do we not all love the Welsh mountains and do we not rush to find our own peace and religion amongst their rocky peaks? Think instead of the romantic splendour of Snowdonia; the magnificence of the snow dusted, brittle-crusted Carneddau on some hard cold winter's morning; a sun bleeding cochineal on the Glyders, iced like some badly done wedding cake; large and simple, colours running . . . And when the sun shines, is not the Welsh sky the truest blue ever? There will be curlews calling as you trudge over sheep-cropped springy moss and heather, up to your chosen rock climb or mountain summit, and you will probably remark that there is no finer place to be. You will be right of course. North Wales is the definitive romantic experience whether it be on the mountains, the crags, the castles or beaches. Oh yes, there are castles; grey crumbling myth-bound places. Or take a walk along Newborough Beach one November evening – it must be November – as the wind whips the sand and carries it knee high scratching and howling. Snatch the odd glance across the Straits towards the cloud-held mountains . . . and then deny that you are moved by it all . . .

And what of the rock? Well, there are testpieces a-plenty. Fierce gymnastic examinations at which the rock tigers, and the little cubs, will throw themselves, body and soul, full pelt. Apart from the short technical problems, there are still the bold, lonely quests to be had. Self-analysis on Cloggy, adventures on Gogarth and discos in Llanberis.

Wales has got the lot. There are big hills to walk up and if you think walking up hills is boring, then you are probably under 25, have no soul, and don't fully appreciate the spiritual significance of rain storms, although I admit there are times when the thrill of wearing damp knickers wears thin.

If you don't wish to plod up hills, you can take the train to the top. At the time of writing there is only one railway station operating in the mountains (most trains stop at Bangor), but no doubt we shall soon gasp in admiration at the sight and sound of locomotive advances in other areas. Aah . . . such is progress! Such is man's desire to scale the highest peaks . . .

NB: it is worth noting that the train to Snowdon has been successfully 'hitched'. To gain membership to The Hitch-hikers Club, the three necessary hitches are (1) a train, (2) a hearse, and (3) some kind or aviation transporter, such as helicopter or glider, although rescues are not acceptable.

Description of the Main Climbing Areas

The area divisions below are those used by Paul Williams in one of his guidebooks *Snowdonia Rock Climbs*. Paul is wonderful for his age and, I am told, still has periods of lucidity. I remember with great fondness the Christmases he spent with the Fawcett household. He was particularly moved by my Christmas pudding, as indeed we all were.

The Llanberis Area
Snowdon South
Snowdon North
Carneddau and Ogwen
North Coast limestone
Craig Gogarth

However, the ones I have used are as follows:

The Llanberis area including slate
Tremadog
Idwal Slabs
Pentrwyn

The Llanberis Area

There are two parts to the area, both integral to the Llanberis experience. Firstly there is the town itself where the 'scene' happens and secondly there are the surrounding hills where the climbing takes place.

The town, the collection of buildings, affectionately known as Beris, is a strange bleak hole, a perfect example of a depressed area set against the magnificent backdrop of Snowdonia.

Several years ago I was invited, as representative of the BUMS, to an annual dinner by some other club. After being suitably patronized all evening I was waiting at the bus stop in the town to return from whence I had come. It was a cold grey Sunday morning. A light drizzle added interest to my wait. Newspaper pages from a discarded fish supper travelled in a higgledy-piggledy windswept fashion along the glistening pavement, pausing occasionally to attach themselves to the odd pile of muck. It was a thoughtful time for me. Two local youths passed by and shouted something in Welsh. They were cheerful and laughed loudly at the joke. I think it was me. This miserable scene was further enhanced by the arrival of a thin, yellow-eyed mongrel limping down the middle of the high street. It was lame. It is a scene that has stayed with me a long time. Sometimes I have nightmares . . . However, the climbing is 'where it's at' and offers something for everyone. It epitomizes the divisions between the old and new trends in the climbing world. The Pass is steeped in History and Tradition. Incredibly old climbers like Joe Brown used to practise techniques here, like being hard, and one line put downs, but that was before he became a singer and quiz show host. I liked him best on Blankety Blank when he said something amusing.

However, I digress. The pass is Traditional and only very old climbers and outdoor centres go there. You will need your waterproofs and big boots. There are stacks of classics to do and you can say things like, 'My goodness, how on earth did the early pioneers get up this route with their primitive equipment?' (Answer, they were much better climbers than you'll ever be!)

Slate

The modern end of the climbing game is exemplified by the activities in the slate quarries surrounding Llanberis, recently renamed Paul Williams Quarries! in honour of Cwm Y Glo's most adopted son. Paul has been responsible for much activity on slate. All the climbs have been cleaned, led and seconded by Paul who reproduces by cloning. You can enter the contest to spot the difference. If you think you've found the genuine article, confront him, carrying a copy of *Snowdonia Rock* and say the magic words, 'Eh up'. If it is Paul, the correct response will be 'Eh up youth'. You can then claim your free insult.

Mr Williams, known to his mother as Paul, is the chief protaganist of the Slate Movement which has only recently taken off, attracting devotees from all over the country, although nowhere is this fanaticism more strongly felt than amongst the Llanberis habitués.

The slate movement started off as something very beautiful. It was a way of expressing a vision, of stating in the simplest terms the climbing feeling, and also a good way of getting some very rude words into print via the new route name, which is often little more than descriptions

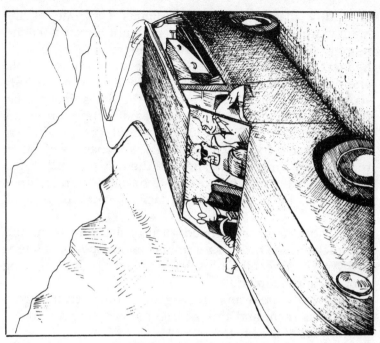

of bodily discharges. Paul Williams was one of the main instigators of 'the movement' – not merely a leader, more of a driving force for the younger generation who had lost their way and needed to be shown how to bolt, and chip good holds. 'Chipideedodah', a beautifully sculptured jug, Paul's statement of the times, is a perfect illustration, a summing up, a reaffirmation of man's mastery of the rock. No longer would young climbers have to search for holds, to scan vast expanses of blank rock looking for the 'line', instead the way forward would be impeded only by the individual's own failings whether it be limited vision, lack of spirit or a small chisel.

As Paul, the unrecognized guru of the movement and chronicler of the times, said in his famous speech, 'Slate of the Art', before an uninvited audience: 'Clip in, Dog around, and Drop off.'

Paul was a spokesman for a generation, even though it wasn't his own, and this phrase perfectly expressed the sentiments of the time.

Paul's subtle use of tact and delicate expressions amazed and entranced all who heard him. Slate prospered and many were attracted to this strange modern medium, and also the rock. Of course, human nature being what it is, the inevitable happened; there were renegades. Climbers called Trevor veered away from the light and set off on their own perverted path, routes were climbed solo, or with spaced gear, or even on sight. The subsequent adulation of the misguided masses has lead to an increase in this deviant behaviour. The vision has gone rotten. A whole generation, forgetting the lessons of the past, is ignoring the chipped hold, the convenient bolt, the re-hearsed moves and is instead 'going for it' once more. No good will come of it, mark my words, there'll be tears, as my mother used to say when she was smacking me around the head with the coal skuttle.

So what of the present situation? Well, the old classics remain to taunt the young pups. I've seen the skinnies gazing in awe at 'Colossus', the Master's work of art, desperately trying to understand the route description, then struggling to solve the problem start. It's a question of weight. How to carry the necessary 86 krabs and still get off the ground?

(They might be able to do 6c moves 40 feet out from an RP1, imminent ground fall, but how often do you see them on placing gear on a 5a? Soloing? . . . Yes, but placing gear? . . . No.)

Slate is a different game. It is smooth, sparsely protected and prone to snapping holds. Small wonder then that its devotees, the Slate Heads, are found in the quarries (lying at the bottom moaning) or in Bangor General (lying in Ward 3 moaning) or in the pub (lying on the floor moaning).

The most likely venue for evening moaning is the Padarn.

Tremadog
What a friendly alternative to the sombre wet mountain experience of Snowdonia! An easy-angled playground for the classic bagger and also some tricky hard stuff with interesting names. 'Strawberries' with the direct finish named 'Dream Topping' illustrates perfectly the zany word play among today's top climbers!!

The crag is a popular choice for Welsh climbing when it is raining in the Pass, it makes a pleasant change to sit in Eric's Café rather than Pete's Eats. The climbing is very close to the road and the local council have done it very nicely so that you can walk along the bottom and watch the climbers. A pair of binoculars are useful for the really dedicated climber-watcher. There's no way to fail anonymously here, so tread carefully.

Idwal Slabs

The Idwal Slabs, in the Ogwen Valley, have been the
starting ground for many climbers. The great grey sweep
of granite attracts beginners like muck does flies. Here
they come in all weathers with cagoules, big boots and
sacks for a wet day's queuing on Hope and Tennis Shoe.
Stamina and determination are of the essence as the rain
seeps quickly through those new orange waterproofs and
the climber in front gets stuck on the easy part.

Here, in the Carneddau, it is still possible to serve a
proper apprenticeship getting wet and miserable, de-
veloping the qualities of bloody-mindedness and mean
temper necessary for the greater ranges. You won't get
that sort of character-building in the South of France!

Pentrwyn

THE GREAT ORME, LLANDUDNO

Once upon a time the cream of British climbing gathered
here. It was boom time, new routes were climbed inces-
santly and restrictions were unheard of. People stayed at
the crags for weeks at a time, sleeping rough in the caves
and breakfasting at Mrs P's. Notables, such as Andy
'Thunder Thighs' Pollitt and Jerry 'This is the fastest road
bike money can buy' Moffat, were regularly observed
doing things.

Pentrwyn was 'the' place to climb in the summer of
1983, bolts were placed every two or three minutes, chalk
fell like snow, jokes were told, songs were sung and a
carnival atmosphere prevailed. Everyone was very supportive. There were no 'angry young men' here, the
occasional tantrum maybe, the odd stamping of pretty
little feet and an infrequent pout, but very rarely did I
glimpse a bottom lip tremble or an eye moisten, and then
only with good cause, such as snagged tights or lost

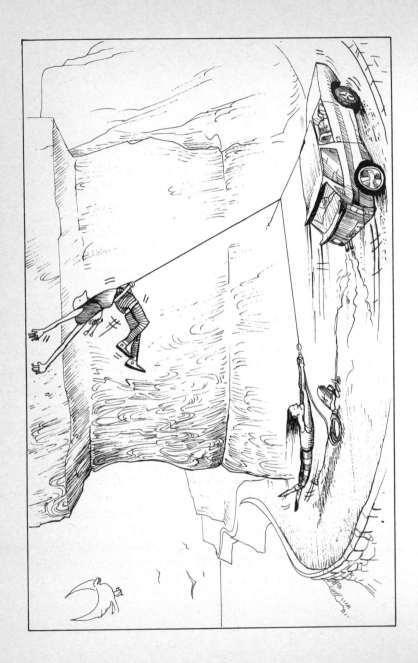

earrings. The Jimmy Porters of the climbing world were absent . . .

The construction of the crag is such that the Marine driveway runs directly below the climbing. Consequently elderly tourists will stop to watch the antics, give themselves heart attacks, and us the benefit of their experience: 'You must be barmy. You wouldn't catch me doing that' (rather obvious really).

One passerby inadvertently named one of the area's most well-known climbs.

Ron was making the first ascent of a route. I was belaying – for a change – and chatting to Paul Williams. An elderly gentleman stopped, looked up at Ron, and commented, 'That looks very hard.'

'It is,' said Paul.

'Is he good?' asks the old chap.

'Oh yes,' said Paul.

'Is he as good as Hillary?' queries our new friend.

'As good as Hillary? He's better than him. That's Charlton Chestwig! He's the greatest climber in the world!'

'Oh right ho,' says our friend and gazes in awe at 'Charlton' doing his stuff.

And so 'Charlton Chestwig The World's Greatest Climber' weighed in at a hefty E5 6b.

Since those days the flavour has changed. There are various rules in operation which restrict climbing hours and, given the proximity of the tourists and their vehicles, it is a necessary precaution. The sea air has eroded much of the in-situ protection giving an air of uncertainty to many climbs. Who wants to climb on rotting bolts? The café scene at Mrs P's altered as newcomers took advantage of the relaxed atmosphere. Things ain't what they were!

How strange to feel nostalgia for a time passed only a couple of years ago. Time moves on . . .

Pubs

THE BLACK LION
LLANFAIR TALHAIARN
ABERGELE
CLWYD LL22 8R7
Telephone: (074584) 205

Mine Hosts are Don and Glenys Livingstone. The pub is found by
taking the A548 from Abergele (the Llanrwst road).

BEER
The pub is a Robinsons pub.

FOOD
Bar snacks and restaurant food are available and veggies are OK. The
menu varies from sausage and chips at £1.25 to 8 oz sirloin (a
vegetarian special?) at £5.25, with traditional Sunday lunch served on
traditional Sundays. Serving times are up to 2.30 p.m.(ish) on weekdays and 1.30 p.m.(ish) on Sundays. The evening servings are until
9.30 p.m. or until the chips run out.

FACILITIES
There is a pool table, dart board for chucking darts at and public
telephone. Children are allowed in, but small hairy four-legged child
substitutes are not. Muddy boots are OK in the vault which used to be
the 'men only' card room way back before the women's liberation
movement hit Abergele last Thursday. The vault room is now used
mainly by farmers for complaining about poverty, and drinking.

There are caravan and camping facilities nearby and fishing in the
river outside the pub. The pub is well used by climbers and enjoys a
good reputation. It is recommended in other guides and the landlord is
particularly jolly.

Clwyd Mountaineering Club meet here on the first Wednesday of
the month between 7.30 p.m. and 8.00 p.m.

BRYN TYRCH HOTEL
CAPEL CURIG
GWYNEDD LL24 0EL
Telephone: (06904) 223

Mine Host is Peter Davies. The pub is on the main A5 road from Capel
Curig.

BEER
Beers on offer include Flowers and Castle Eden.

126

FOOD
Bar snacks are served from 12.00 to 2.15 p.m. at dinnertime and from 7.00 p.m. to 9.45 p.m. in the evening.

FACILITIES
Dogs are allowed if well behaved. Children are allowed if well behaved.

OPINION
An excellent alternative to the regular Capel watering holes. Conducive landlord.

COBDENS HOTEL
CAPEL CURIG
BETWS Y COED
GWYNEDD
Telephone: (06904) 243

BEER
Tetleys, Youngers.

FOOD
Food is served and varies according to the room you choose. There is a bar menu in the back room which consists of things with chips. Service is not fast.

FACILITIES
These include a pool table (is it sloping, or is it me?) and a juke box which is excellent. Hands up all the Doris Day fans!

Everyone seems to have spent some part of their adolescence here. I myself spent several hours one summer evening with a small group of well-behaved, quiet friends. It was a beautiful evening and all available ground was occupied by day trippers, families, a few climbers. As dusk fell, a woman screamed. What could it be we wondered? And there, running down the middle of the A5 was Strappo. Apart from being completely naked, not too surprising to those who know him, he had painted himself in luminescent green paint. That *was* surprising. In the failing light he looked remarkably like a glowing skeleton racing down the street. Small children pointed. I did too. Thinking back, it wasn't that warm, even for summer . . .

There are two bars to choose from, the back bar being the 'climbers' bar' and being well known amongst the fraternity. It is a desperate spot, aspiring hopelessly to be basic. The stone floor perfectly complements the back wall of the room which is the rock face, slate as a matter of interest. In theory the idea is quite romantic, duplicating the Welsh mountain experience; the rock, a small stream, small clumps of

Cobden's Back Bar, North Wales

heather, etc. The reality is a little different. Who in their right minds wants to sit in a cold dripping hole? I can do that at home. Actually you might as well go the whole way and try caving, at least you get to take your clothes off in public afterwards.

There is lots of atmosphere; all the hilarity and carefree abandon of a funeral wake.

As if all this weren't enough, the tables are wobbly to help you spill your beer over yourself. Try another pub.

THE DOUGLAS ARMS (Worth a Visit)
HIGH STREET
BETHESDA
NR BANGOR
GWYNEDD LL57 3BY
Telephone: (0248) 600219

Mine Host is Geoff and the Douggie Arms is found on the left-hand side of the main street, as you head for the hills.

BEER
The beer on offer is Marstons and local beers. There is a very extensive whisky choice; the cleaner said there were probably 64 different labels.

FOOD
Rolls only are served but these are OK.

FACILITIES
There is a games room, full-size snooker table, dart board and public phone. Dogs are allowed and kids are OK at lunchtime. Muddy boots are OK. No singing.

OPINION
This pub is popular with climbers and has a great atmosphere if, like me, you're into other people's living rooms. Apart from the decor, the other notable feature is that business transactions are carried out in old money, none of that new-fangled decimal currency here, although your modern money will be accepted graciously. Still no singing.

THE GOLDEN FLEECE INN
MARKET SQUARE
TREMADOG
PORTHMADOG
Telephone: Porthmadog 512421

Mine Host is Roger Jones and the pub is on the main road from Porthmadog to Beddgelert/Caernarfon.

BEER
The Fleece is a free house.

FOOD
Bar snacks and restaurant food are served at dinnertime from 12.00 to 2.30 p.m. and at teatime from 7.00 p.m. to 9.45 p.m. Vegetarian food is offered. The menu offers sausage and chips at £1.30, to salmon at £6.50.

FACILITIES
These include a pool table during the winter. No dogs or muddy boots, although children are accommodated. There is a covered courtyard for climbers and the pub is recommended in food and beer guides.

HALFWAY HOUSE
PORT DINORWIG
NR CAERNARFON
GWYNEDD
NORTH WALES
Telephone: (0248) 670240

Mine Host is Mr Portillo.

BEER
The pub is an Ansells pub.

FOOD
Bar meals are on sale between 12.00 and 2.15 p.m. (on Sunday 1.45 p.m.) and between 6.30 p.m. and 9.30 p.m. Monday to Saturday. Food ranges from sandwiches at £1, steak at £6.50, four vegetarian dishes and lasagne.

FACILITIES
These comprise a games room and public telephone. No dogs are allowed in when food is served. Children are OK up to 8.30 p.m. Muddy boots are OK. Plas Menai is close by.

COMMENT
'Highly recommended.'

THE KINGS HEAD (Worth a Visit)
OLD ROAD
LLANDUDNO
NORTH WALES LL30 2NB
Telephone: (0492) 77993

Mine Host is Mr P. R. Smith and the pub is situated near to the tram station.

BEER
An Ansells pub.

FOOD
Restaurant food and a few snacks are on offer. These are served every day between 12.00 and 2.30 p.m. and from 7.00 p.m. to 10.30 p.m. except Christmas. (Skiving off eh?) Vegetarian dishes are occasionally served.

FACILITIES
Dogs are allowed in the pub, but not the restaurant. Children are OK, but no muddy boots. There is a public telephone. Camping is 5 miles away, or the town is riddled with B&Bs, or there is camping *au sauvage*, i.e. dossing with the sheep under the crags.

OPINION
Recommended in *Good Food Guide* and *Les Routiers*. Friendly ladies behind the bar. Although this isn't much frequented by climbers, it is worth a visit.

THE PADARN LAKE HOTEL
LLANBERIS
SNOWDONIA LL55 4SU
Telephone: (0286) 870260 (management)/870204 (bar)

BEER
Bass.

FOOD
Serving times are 12.00 to 2.00 p.m. seven days a week.

FACILITIES
These include a bar snack menu with a separate restaurant serving à la carte. A pool table and dart board. Overnight accommodation is available.

OPINION
This is probably the most well-known and frequented drinking spot in Llanberis and has seen some substantial alterations over the last few years due to it having been completely rebuilt. However, to those of us old fogeys whose memory banks are still operative, the old Padarn had a quaint charm, reminiscent of a large public lavatory. Features at that time included a vicious parrot that was perched above the off-sales, ready to hack bloody chunks out of any light-fingered customers. You could stand ankle deep in slops and jostle in a jocular fashion with the

many stars that drank there. (This is in the pre-Training era when you could drink and still be a rock star, I'm going back a few years now . . .) You could push, respectfully of course, past Joe Brown playing darts to get to the gents' loo. All this has changed now. The dart board is in the wrong position and Mr Brown might think it rather odd if you started rubbing up against him, saying you were only trying to go to the toilet.

Now we are in the 1980s and it's obvious that 'money has changed hands' to cater for a clientele far removed from the bearded weathered check-shirted drunken climbing fraternity. There are carpets! Plush velour seats! Hovering bar staff in ties! Despite all this, the pub remains a focal point for the scene in Llanberis. We climbers are determined folk and will not be intimidated by slow service and hygienic conditions. United we stand! Divided we fall!

The old barn has now been split into two. A back bar serves us and a lounge bar caters for the rest of the world. This point is made by a notice asking climbers and walkers to confine their debauched antics to the other room. (OK so it doesn't actually spell it out, but we girls can take a hint can't we?)

The lounge bar features plastic flowers and pretentious Welsh posters. Entertainment is provided on Wednesday, Friday and Saturday nights, courtesy of Morgan on the Organ. To be fair to the proprietors, something of the original character has been retained by way of the smell at the entrance. A charming detail.

PEN Y GWRYD HOTEL (Worth a Visit)
NANTGWYNANT
CAERNARFON
GWYNEDD
NORTH WALES LL55 4NT
Telephone: (0286) 870211/870768

Mine Hosts are Mr and Mrs C. B. Briggs and Mr and Mrs B. C. Pullee and the hotel is situated at the junction of the A4086 and the A498 at the top end of the Llanberis Pass.

BEER
The PYG is a free house.

FOOD
Both bar snacks and restaurant food are served. Bar snacks are served between the hours of 12.00 and 2.00 p.m. The dining room only is open from 7.30 p.m. to 8.00 p.m. in the evening, so you've got to be quick. The menu changes every day and costs about £9.50. Vegetarians are accepted.

FACILITIES
These include a games room, pool table, a dart board and a public telephone, all of which are for resident guests only. However, dogs, children and muddy boots are allowed on the slate floors of the public bars.

According to the management, 'the Pen Y Gwryd is the home of British mountaineering' and is famous for its connection with the successful 1953 expedition. No doubt it was here, in the bar, that our brave lads had the idea of bagging a peak. Things don't change do they? You know how it is, anything seems possible after a few pints.

The interior is done out in dark wood and the coal fires provide comfort. The overall impression is of a log cabin, warm and welcoming. The atmosphere is Very Traditional with an assortment of ancient climbing gear and yellowing photographs decorating the ceiling and walls. An old rope (actually it doesn't look too bad), several pairs of clinkers and a pair of Mallory's old underpants emphasize the long-standing association between this pub and the mountaineering world.

The hotel offers accommodation and on the other side of the bar is a room for guests only. There seems to be some kind of cabinet display of historical memorabilia. You can peer over the bar and gaze from a respectful distance at various old guidebooks, climbing equipment and ageing guests.

SARACEN'S HEAD HOTEL
BEDDGELERT
GWYNEDD
NORTH WALES LL55 4UY
Telephone: (076 686) 223

Mine Host is Alan Scott.

BEER
The pub is tied to Robinsons.

FOOD
Bar snacks are served from 11.00 a.m. to 3.00 p.m. and from 5.30 p.m. to 10.30 p.m. Restaurant food is served from 12.00 to 2.00 p.m. and from 7.00 p.m. to 9.00 p.m. Tea, coffee and sandwiches are also available from 9.30 a.m. to 11.00 a.m. and from 3.00 p.m. to 5.00 p.m. Veggies are pandered to.

FACILITIES
There is a games room, a pool table, dart board, telephone, and dogs, kids and muddy boots are all embraced. B&B is available from £14.

COMMENT
'Worth a visit.'

TYN Y COED (Recommended)
CAPEL CURIG
BETWS Y COED
GYWNEDD
Telephone: 331

Mine Host is George F. Wainwright.

BEER
The pub is a free house serving Castle Eden, and is found on the A5 about 1 mile from Capel Curig.

FOOD
Both bar snacks and restaurant food are served at dinnertime between 12.00 and 2.30 p.m., and in the evenings between 6.30 p.m. and 9.30 p.m. Veggies are placated and the menu is fairly extensive, reasonably priced and good value.

FACILITIES
These include a pool table and public telephone. Dogs are not allowed in but children are. (Typical!)
   This is one of the most popular pubs with climbers and walkers in the area, and rightly so. The furnishings are pleasant and very conducive with open fires and pine-clad toilets. There is sufficient seating for large parties. It is rumoured that John Barry favours this pub, but despite that it's worth a visit.

THE VAYNOL ARMS (Worth a Visit)
NANT PERIS
GWYNEDD
NORTH WALES LL55 4UF
Telephone: (0286) 870284

Mine Hosts are Emlyn and Marie Baylis. The pub is situated on the A4086 at the bottom of the Llanberis Pass.

BEER
The pub is tied to Robinsons.

FOOD
Bar snacks are served during the summer between 12.00 and 2.30 p.m. at dinnertime and 6.30 p.m. to 9.30 p.m. in the evening. During the winter the times are 12.00 to 2.00 p.m. and 7.00 p.m. to 9.00 p.m. Vegetarians are catered for via the lasagne and you can get coffee.

FACILITIES
There is a pool table, a juke box, a dart board (I've spent many contented hours trying to focus on double top), a public telephone and,

The Vaynol Arms, North Wales

round the back, there is a public swing park so you can play silly devils at closing time. Dogs are not allowed in, but children are and I know which I'd rather have. Muddy boots are acceptable in the climbers' bar.

The Vaynol is also recommended in the *Good Beer Guide* and although there is no accommodation, there is camping directly opposite and a five-minute walk leads to the infamous Humphreys bunkhouse . . .

OPINION

I like this pub very much and have spent many evenings relaxing here. (I don't get drunk, I get relaxed as do my legs which is why walking is such a problem.) However, I am not alone in my appreciation and the Vaynol is a popular pub. A traditional climbers' watering hole, much loved by traditional climbers. All very jolly, sweaty and hairy. Much good-natured pushing and shoving to get served. A useful tip is to kick the person in front of you on the back of the knees. As they collapse instantaneously below the bar, then . . . wallop . . . you're in . . . 'Two pints of your finest, landlord, in a proper man's glass if you don't mind. Thank you,' there you are then, well on your way to oblivion.

It is also a safe place to drink. I have deduced from the number of striped jumpers, radio transmitters and tough expressions that members of the local Mountain Rescue frequent this establishment so the danger of avalanche is probably minimal. They know about these things.

Cafés

ANCASTER MILK BAR
BETWS Y COED
NORTH WALES
Telephone: (06902) 505

OPENING TIMES
The café is open from 10.00 a.m. to about 5.00 p.m. and on Sundays from 10.00 a.m. to about 7.00 p.m.

Snacks, toasties and things with chips are available, vegetarian dishes are not.

COMMENT
'Highly recommended.'

ERIC'S CAFÉ
BWLCH Y MOCH FILLING STATION
TREMADOG
NR PORTHMADOG
Telephone: (0766) 512199

The proprietor is Eric Jones, the Sean Connery of the climbing world.

OPENING TIMES
During the winter months up to Easter, the café opens at weekends from 9.00 a.m. to 6.00 p.m.(ish). From June onwards they open all week.

FACILITIES
These include camping, plus tea in bed, and a climbers' barn which lends itself to indoor climbing. The café also sells magazines, some climbing equipment and guidebooks.

HAPPY VALLEY CAFÉ
HAPPY VALLEY
LLANDUDNO
NORTH WALES
Telephone: (0492) 75364

The proprietress is Mrs Parisella and the café is often known as Mrs P's or Parisellas.

OPENING TIMES
These are from between 9.00 and 9.30 a.m. to about 5.30 p.m. depending on the weather.
   The food on offer in winter ranges from sandwiches, pasties, sausage rolls, and in the summer it's chips with things.

OPINION
Popular with tourists, but the nearest café to the crags at Pentrwyn and worth a visit.

OGWEN FALLS SNACK BAR
NR BETHESDA
GWYNEDD
NORTH WALES

This permanent structure in the car park near the Youth Hostel replaces the old tea shack, a haven of tea and comfort in the driving rains of those grotty Freshers' meets. (This is going back a bit now when novice climbers went to such places to serve their apprenticeships. Nowadays this fun period is completely omitted as pubescent youths/youthesses head straight for the South of France. Honestly, they don't know what they're missing.)
   The snack bar serves a large selection of food and drinks and is also licensed to sell alcohol – beer and wine – which might be just the thing after a day on the hills. It is rather pricey though, which is inevitable. The service is very efficient and the public loos are next door, which is handy.

PETE'S EATS (Highly Recommended)
HIGH STREET
LLANBERIS
GWYNEDD LL55 4EU
Telephone: (0286) 870 358

The Proprietors are the Nortons, Pete and Vicky.

OPENING TIMES
The café is open seven days a week, except Christmas, which is fair enough. From Monday to Friday between the hours of 9.00 a.m. to 6.30 p.m., and on Saturdays and Sundays from 8.00 a.m. to 8.00 p.m.

FOOD
What can I say? The menu is extensive, offering almost everything an outdoor person could want; big plates and good helpings. There is a vegetarian menu for the eco-freaks, including a range of herbal teas. (What's going on here? Talk about pampering! Whatever happened to the climbers' number two favourite refreshment; proper tea? It should be dark, strong and well brewed; brackish in taste, but better than drinking mud.)

THE BIASED OPINION
At last! The mecca for café buffs. The ultimate climbers' café, satisfying all the basic requirements: long opening hours, good value food, reasonably quick service and well-known climbers to gawp at. The stripped pine interior is almost yuppie until the customers are in. I shall be kind and say that Pete's attracts a range of types. Tasteful touches with the green gloss paintwork and matching tablecloths.

It is clean and friendly, there are many climbing photographs to look at, you may even spot yourself featured, although I didn't. The notice board is filled with interesting notices about self-help groups; hardly surprising really. Eye-catching headlines like:
'MAYBE I'M PREGNANT . . .'
    ('Or maybe I'm just a big, fat piggy')
'NEED HELP?'   ('Yes')
'FRIENDSHIP?'   ('Oh yes')
'ADVICE?'   ('Yes Yes . . .')
'THEN CONTACT LLANBERIS EXIT . . .'
and
'DRUGS, MAIM AND KILL' which I took to be some kind of initiation procedure for living in the area, until I re-read it as,
'DRUGS MAIM AND KILL'
What a difference a comma makes! There is also a phone number for grassing on your mates which is a nice idea.

There are climbing notices in abundance, an advert offers a knotting service for old ropes. A yellowing envelope, postmarked 1981, for some

Pete's Eats, North Wales

poor soul who never returned from that fateful expedition ... or maybe he is now married with two kids, a stripped pine interior and wok, living in the real world again.

FACILITIES
These include magazines and newspapers to read, a juke box, a public telephone complete with useful telephone numbers, and a non-smokers room.

(Have I gushed enough, Pete?)

THE PINNACLE CAFÉ
CAPEL CURIG
GWYNEDD
NORTH WALES

OPENING TIMES
From 8.45 a.m. to 5.30 p.m., and later in the summer.

I include this café in case you get stuck, hitching at Capel. The main grocery store leads through to a small café area. They cater for the tourists, with cakes and fancies, but a pot of tea for 30p is OK. The nearest toilet is round the back of Joe Brown's shop, which isn't impressive. One of the main reasons I end up in cafés is to use their toilets.

THE SNOWDONIA CAFÉ (Highly Recommended)
CAPEL CURIG
GWYNEDD
NORTH WALES
Telephone: (Capel Curig) 246

OPENING HOURS
The times of opening are extensive; all year round except Christmas. In winter, weekends from 7.00 a.m. to 8.30 p.m. and during the week from 8.00 a.m. to 7.00 p.m. During the summer they are open from 6.00 a.m. to 11.00 p.m. At that rate they deserve to make a bob or two.

The Snowdonia is situated on the A5 a mile from Capel. It's just what we want; nothing flash – clean, friendly, reasonably priced and the service is good. There are facilities for eating outside which is highly recommended in summer.

The café is perched up several flights of steps which gets the blood rushing back to the much abused cortex. However, the view on a clear day is well worth a small headache. What could be finer than tucking into a hearty English breakfast of bacon and eggs whilst gazing out, past the comprehensive cactus display, towards Snowdon, anticipating the day's activities ahead? Get a good gaze in, since the mountain can be completely covered in cloud and lost in the mists of Welshness by the time you've slopped ketchup on your fried bread. The weather changes pretty quickly in these parts.

The toilets are fine; basic but with soft paper.

OTHER FACILITIES
Bunkhouse accommodation is available at £1.50 a night.

Places to Stay

HUMPHREY'S BARN
NANT PERIS
LLANBERIS
GWYNEDD
NORTH WALES
Telephone: (0286) 870356

Humphrey's is situated about half a mile up the Llanberis Pass from Nant Peris.

The barn costs £1 per person per night and has eighteen bunks, so it probably sleeps about 54. You need your own sleeping and cooking gear. Camping is also available in the small field opposite the house.

OPINION
Well, who hasn't stayed here at some time during their outdoor careers? The kind of place where the memory lingers long after the experience has passed.

There is a quaint custom here that separate sleeping quarters are maintained for members of the various sexes, the main sleeping area being reserved for the men, and so it was that two lady friends and I found ourselves arriving, in all innocence and unobserved, in the barn at 11.30 p.m. Finding, to our discomfort, someone had forgotten their sleeping bag, we decided to double up as only close friends can. It was hard enough, the next morning, explaining our female presences in the male domain, but the old dear nearly had a cardiac arrest on seeing two feminine heads in a sleeping bag made for one. In the ensuing outrage, I think we may have escaped without paying.

Tourist Information

Tourist information is available from several information centres which are situated at the following addresses:

National Park Information Centre
The Wharf
Aberdyfi

National Park Information Centre
High Street
Bala

National Park Information Centre
Royal Oak Stables
Betws-Y-Coed

National Park Information Centre
Isallt
Church Street
Blaenau Ffestiniog

National Park Information Centre
Beechwood House
Dolgellau

National Park Information Centre
Gwyddfor House
High Street
Harlech

NB: postal enquiries are dealt with from the National Park Office at
Penrhyndeudraeth.

North Wales Weather

Information on ground conditions, plus a daily forecast, can be
obtained by ringing (0286) 870120. This is now a recorded message,
although there was a time when ringing this number was luck of the
draw.

A cleaner once answered a query with the response, 'Hang on, I'll
just go and have a look . . . er . . . it doesn't look very nice.'

The North Wales Appendix

Pubs

THE BULL
DEINIOLEN
NR LLANBERIS

COMMENT
'Most people tend to steer clear of this pub because they claim it has a
Welsh Nationalist atmosphere, but the pub is OK.'

COTTAGE LOAF
LLANDUDNO
NORTH WALES

COMMENTS
OK. Sited in the town by the market hall.

THE GEORGE
BLACK DIAMOND STREET
CHESTER

Chester M.C. meet here through the winter on Wednesday evenings at
8.30 p.m.

THE GREIG INN
PONTFADOG

COMMENT
'Very good, conducive landlord.' Handy for Pandy Rocks in the Glyn
Ceiriog Valley.

THE PLOUGH INN
PONTESBURY

COMMENT
'Half a mile from the crag but the nicest atmosphere.'

THE PUB AT RHYD DHU
NR BEDDGELERT

COMMENT
'Highly recommended, although very crowded on Saturdays. Good
food and beer.'

THE ROBINSONS PUB IN LLANDEGAI

COMMENT
'Highly recommended.'

THE WATERLOO HOTEL
BETWS Y COED

Clwyd M.C. meet here on Sundays from 6.00 p.m. onwards. (6.00 p.m.!
That's the spirit!)

Chip Shops
SHREWSBURY CHIP SHOP

'Follow the signs from the A5 to the town centre, turning left at a roundabout. 3–400 yards on the right, immediately after the railway, there is a small chip shop. The café part is open until 10.30 p.m. on Fridays. Parking is easy.'

Pembroke

I shall let you into a secret. Not many people know this but there are actually two Pembrokes. There is 'Pembroke' and then there is the more well-known 'Pembroke-at-Easter'. A typical conversation might run: 'Where are you off to this holiday? . . . What? . . . You must be joking! . . . You're going to Pembroke-at-Easter! Crikey!'

Pembroke and Pembroke-at-Easter are two different places. First of all:

Pembroke-at-Easter

At this time of year the place is full of climbers. It's bonkers. Last time I was there I counted 967 climbers. This was reduced to 965½ in the afternoon. Easter-climbing in Pembroke is DANGEROUS. You can hurt yourself. What's more to the point, other people can hurt you. This is done in a variety of ways such as falling, or dropping rocks, on your head. It isn't very subtle but it's damned effective. Be warned!

The Climbing

Whereas Cornwall is the holiday focus for climbers leading up to VS, Pembroke is the place for those climbing at

145

Pembroke at Easter

HVS and above. The main feature about Pembroke is that it is completely flat until you reach the edge, it then drops sharply, vertically actually, into the sea via 100 feet of rock which you and I then spend several hours trying to get to the top of. Having surmounted the difficulties presented by one ascent, we then start all over again somewhere else. What complex creatures we climbers are!

Climbers come to Pembroke to have a good time. There is a refreshing lack of angry young men out to prove things. There are, however, quite a few jolly old climbers proving things, such as 'a stinking hangover doesn't make you climb better'. It's good to see the old 'uns getting out and shaking a leg, particularly on the rock.

As for the weather, the sun is always up there and shining – it's just that sometimes the wind and rain are more obvious. It's all a question of how you look at these things.

Clothing is quite relaxed and anything is acceptable so long as it's not flash. Ron Hill bottoms are the trendiest things seen. When it gets very hot, rolled up Ron Hills are just the thing for the older climber. At the height of summer, the attire for the smart holiday climber is Ron Hill shorts, Ron Hill string vest, peaked cap and doodle-buggers. The potential new-router should carry a bucket and spade for gardening climbs and building sand castles.

Climbing here is not just a matter of picking a route and doing it; there are restrictions because of birds nesting and because our brave lads use certain areas as target practice. It's a great comfort to know that when the button is pressed, our boys will be able to miss derelict tanks by only a few yards. Of course, if you choose to ignore the red warning flags, you run the risk of confrontation with members of Her Majesty's Armed Forces. Apparently they shoot blanks, so you don't have to worry about precautions.

The Socializing

If you are lonely, then a trip here will provide several social encounter points. For example:

1 Abseiling down other people's ropes. Don't ask permission and sooner or later a climber will seek you out for a chat.

2 Queuing for routes. Choose a 3 star E3 or E4 and you'll have hundreds of people to talk to. Don't worry if you can't climb at that standard, just move away as your turn looms, muttering about the need for solitude and the spiritual search for aloneness, oneness and Zen.

3 Borrowing gear. Climbers leave their gear lying around in messy piles. Try some communal tidiness. If the owner spots you, they'll definitely find time for a quick word of thanks. If no one is around, it's accepted practice to borrow the occasional Rock 8 or Friend 2½. Climbing is a community and are we not all Brothers and Sisters? (If I ever find the Brother who borrowed my Friend 2½, I'll pull his arms and legs off . . . twice . . .)

Unless you are some kind of lonely wierdo, Pembroke-at-Easter can be fully enjoyed, boozing and bullshitting. You can have social interactions in several places, in the privacy of your own Vango on a one-to-one basis, or more likely on a one-to-967 basis in the pub.

Pembroke

Pembroke is very quiet, sshhhh . . .

Pubs

ST GOVANS INN (Recommended)
BOSHERTON
PEMBROKE
SOUTH PEMBROKESHIRE
Telephone: (064681) 311

Pembroke

Mine Hostess is Mrs Sheila Webster. The pub is situated in the village of Bosherton, about 5 miles south west of Pembroke.

BEER
The pub is a free house.

FOOD
Both bar snacks and restaurant food are served between the hours of 12.00 and 3.00 p.m. and between 6.00 p.m. and 10.00 p.m. Vegetarians are catered for.

FACILITIES
There is a pool table, juke box and dart board. Dogs are not allowed in. Children are allowed in for food only. Muddy boots are not allowed in. Accommodation is available at the pub and there is a field for camping in 50 yards away.

This pub is much used by the climbing fraternity and the pub will take telephone messages for climbers.

Restrictions on climbing at Pembroke exist and up-to-date information pamphlets are printed by the Pembrokeshire Coast National Park Authority and distributed in various places, including the St Govans Inn.

OPINION
This is the best pub in the area, being the only one. Because of this monopoly, almost all climbers in the area will visit here. It gets very very busy at Easter, but jolly. I like it. You will have to forgo any pretension of 'private space'. Practise 'squeezing' before arriving; squeezing to the bar and squeezing to the toilet. There is one advantage to a tightly packed pub like this, no matter how drunk you get, it's impossible to fall over.

It's difficult for me to describe the atmosphere of this pub at Easter, since I've never seen more than sweaty armpits and half-full beer glasses.

One feature of Pembrokeshire climbing is the proximity to military firing ranges. Apart from giving our own brave lads a chance to practise, international exchanges take place, a bit like the BMC ones. So don't be surprised if you find yourself drinking alongside a German tank commander in the quiet season.

All in all, the most convenient pub for climbing in this area and a good place for socializing.

Cafés

THE OLDE WORLDE CAFÉ or (Ma Westons) (Highly Recommended)
BOSHERTON
PEMBROKESHIRE
Telephone: (064 681) 216

The Proprietress is Mrs Weston.

OPENING TIMES
The café is open seven days a week from 9.00 a.m. to 7.00 p.m. (approx) and serves mainly snacks, things on toast and cakes.

OPINION
A smashing place although seating is quite limited inside. However, there is plenty of room on the front lawn and few things are finer than sipping tea on a warm evening after a day's scrambling, catching up on the Bosherton gossip.

Tourist Information Centres

Kingsmoor Common
Kilgetty

Tel: Saundersfoot 812175

Open seven days a week.

Harbourmaster's Office
Saundersfoot

Tel: Saundersfoot 811411

Open seven days a week.

The Croft
Tenby

Tel: Tenby 2402

Open seven days a week.

Drill Hall
Main Street
Pembroke

Tel: Pembroke 682148

Not open Sundays.

40 High Street
Haverfordwest

Tel: Haverfordwest 66141

Not open Sundays.

On the National Park Car Park
Broad Haven

Tel: Broad Haven 412

Open seven days a week.

Bank Cottages
Long Street
Newport

Tel: Newport 820912

Open seven days a week.

The City Hall
St David's

Tel: St David's 720392

Open seven days a week.

All the information centres are open from 9.30 a.m. to 5.30 p.m.

More information can be obtained from:
    The Information Officer
    Pembrokeshire Coast National Park
    County Offices
    Haverfordwest
    Dyfed SA61 1QZ

    Tel: Haverfordwest 4591 ext 5135

The Pembroke Appendix

Pubs

THE FERRY INN
PEMBROKE DOCK
PEMBROKESHIRE

Worth a visit for the food. The pub is sited under the bridge.

THE WHITE SWAN
JAMESTON
PEMBROKESHIRE

COMMENT
A recommended pub, popular with climbers staying at May Cottage,
the C.C. hut/house.

Avon

GORDON JENKIN

———◆———

*'What contemptible scoundrel stole the cork from my
lunch?'*

W. C. FIELDS

The Climbing

The Avon Gorge has a love/hate relationship with many
climbers, the endless tales of precarious sloping holds and
distant rotting protection pegs has given the place a
colourful if sometimes exaggerated press. In recent times
much has changed. Avon's derelict ironmongery has
mostly been replaced as well as supplemented by the
addition of that most wonderful of inventions – the bolt.

Climbing wise the gorge splits into three distinctive
parts: the Suspension Bridge Buttress, an attractive
column of natural limestone; the Main Area, Main Wall
and Sea Walls where the quarryman has left amorphous
features of angular stone virtually devoid of anything
resembling a decent crack and finally the Unknown Area
whose Exploding Galaxy Wall provides adventure while
its Upper Wall supplies a popular series of cracks and face
pitches for the Muscle Beach escapist.

Even if good climbing alone does not attract the visitor,
Avon's popularity will doubtless continue. Where else
can you climb on such a clean expanse of quick drying
rock without the inconvenience of leaving town? Where
else can you park at the base of the crag, watch the

Bristol loos, Avon Gorge

boats sail by and listen to the raucous din of passing traffic? Where else in Britain do you get such half decent weather?

Pubs and Cafés

As one might expect with a city crag, food and refreshment is always close to hand. The most immediate facility is Avon's famous (infamous?) tea-wagon sitting in the car park underneath the Main Area. Tea-wagons are one of Britain's culinary institutions and this one lives up to the long tradition of plastic flavoured tea and evil tasting hot-dogs and hamburgers. Years ago the wagon was burnt to the ground, one suspects by a member of its suffering clientele! If the tea proves too much for your palate and beer is needed as quickly as possible then the nearest pubs of any quality are either the Coronation Tap, up in Clifton Village next to the Suspension Bridge, or the Adam and Eve further down the Portway, both about one and a half miles distant. If you are prepared to drive another couple of minutes towards the city centre then The American Eagle, perched on the edge of the round-about opposite from Brunel's other masterpiece, the SS Great Britain, is also worth investigating.

Currently the only regular climbers' pub where one can be sure of finding climbing conversation is the Port of Call atop Blackboy Hill/Whiteladies Road on a Wednes-day night. This is frequented by both the university climbing club and the majority of the more active locals. Blackboy Hill is a useful place to find as it not only has a friendly climbing shop (Brigham's) but also a handy selection of 'eats'. From the tea-wagon take the Portway towards the Suspension Bridge and turn sharp left up the hill (Bridge Valley Road). Follow the road for about half a mile along the edge of the Downs to a roundabout where a right turn leads down Blackboy Hill into Whiteladies

Road and the city centre beyond. The top of Blackboy Hill
has plenty to offer the hungry; three Indian restaurants
and four different takeaways giving a choice of pizzas,
Turkish cooking, Kentucky Fried Chicken and of course
American (for those in need of another hamburger). The
chip shop junkie will no doubt turn right at the zebra
crossing and go along Worrell Road to the Tai Po Chinese
(GREASE – you've seen the film now try the pancake roll).
The Blackboy Café, a kind of upmarket 'Stoney café' has
attractions for some but the best of the lot is probably
Devina's Delicatessen and Diner, a Middle Eastern and
vegetarian spot recently opened to good reviews and
which serves seven days a week until eight or nine at
night.

If it is Wednesday evening and you wish to find the
Port of Call then wander up the short alley next to the
Kings Arms just up from Brigham's. Bristol's other group
of climbers, the Avon Mountaineering Club meet upstairs
on Thursday nights at the Scotsman and his Pack on St
Michaels Hill, located close to the Bristol Royal Infirmary –
another useful place to know!

Pubs

PORT OF CALL (Recommended)
YORK STREET
CLIFTON
BRISTOL
AVON

Mine Hosts are Robin and Frances Nancarrow. The pub is atop
Blackboy Hill/Whiteladies Road (see previous section) and is found by
wandering up the short alley next to the Kings Arms just up from
Brigham's.

BEER
The pub is tied to the Courage Brewery.

FOOD
Bar snacks are available, but only at dinnertime. The menu offers a

choice of bangers and mash at £2, gammon salad and potato at £3, quiche, smoked mackerel and other delicacies, yummy.

FACILITIES
There is a public telephone and a garden for breathing in that fresh summer air . . . cough . . . splutter . . .
   Dogs, children and muddy boots are OK in the garden.

COMMENT
This is the only regular climbers' pub in the area and climbers meet here on a Wednesday night. It is frequented by both the university climbing club and the majority of the more active locals. Recommended.

THE CORONATION TAP (Worth a Visit)
8 SION PLACE
CLIFTON VILLAGE
CLIFTON
BRISTOL BS8 4AX
Telephone: (0272) 739617

Mine Hosts are Mr and Mrs G. Bailey and the pub is found by following the Portway towards the Suspension Bridge and turning sharp left up the hill on Bridge Valley Road. At the top turn right and follow this to Clifton Green. The pub is situated at the bottom of Sion Place on the opposite side of the green right next to the Suspension Bridge. For those on foot it is quicker to walk along the Portway to the Bridge and take a good path up on the right-hand side of the crag.

BEER
The brewery is Courage.

FOOD
Meals are served at lunchtime and, in the evenings if requested and the pub isn't too busy. All the food is homemade and ranges from salads and various specials at £1.60 to 8 oz rump steak at £3.00.

FACILITIES
No children or dogs are allowed, there is a public telephone.

COMMENTS
The Coronation Tap, over 400 years old, is a famous cider house and the only pub in the country that Taunton Cider provide with 22 gallon barrels. It is complete with authentic decor but invariably crowded out with students and tourists – a great place if you like getting legless on strong cider.
   Recommended in the *Good Beer Guide* (CAMRA) and *The Good Pub Guide*.

THE ADAM AND EVE (Worth a Visit)
7 HOPE CHAPEL HILL
HOTWELLS
BRISTOL BS8 4ND
Telephone: (0272) 291508

Mine Host is Richard Cater and the pub is found by following the
Portway along under the Suspension Bridge to The Rose of Denmark
(sited on the right, next to a set of traffic lights). Take the first left, a
narrow street leading uphill, Hope Chapel Hill.

BEER
The pub is tied to the Courage brewery.

FOOD
Bar snacks are served but only at lunchtime.

FACILITIES
Dogs are allowed but no children (a sound strategy!) There is a public
telephone, a juke box, pinball machine and fruit machine.

COMMENTS
The Adam and Eve was once the usual drinking spot for Bristol
climbers, is a much quieter place than the Coronation Tap but still
visited though mostly on wet weekend lunchtimes.
  Recommended in *The Good Pub Guide*.

Cafés

CHEPSTOW

There is a good chip shop in the town centre. The café area is open
until 9.00 p.m. on Fridays. The chip shop part only is open on Sundays.

Cheddar

GORDON JENKIN

—————◆—————

'I can't stand up for falling down'

ELVIS COSTELLO

The Climbing

Cheddar is a unique climbing experience. The gorge is a long, deep chasm whose sheer-sided rock walls feature climbs of up to 400 feet in height. The place has a grandeur unsurpassed by any other inland limestone cliff in Britain, but also a grim, brooding aspect compounded by a luxuriant growth of ivy. Walking along the bottom the climber is crowded in by the enveloping sense of the vertical, all the more daunting when viewed on a typically chill day during the winter months of the permissible climbing season.

Cheddar has a surprisingly complex topology, an unending line of buttresses, gullies, amphitheatres and faces, each with its own individual characteristics and style. Cheddar's best, however, is to be found where the exposure has its greatest bite, the clean open walls where the rock is compact and solid and the situations wildly dramatic. The severe nature of the gorge invariably means that the finest climbs are all in the upper grades. Nevertheless, with over 450 routes to choose from, including some 'big league' stuff, there's plenty to keep all but the most ardent local happy for a considerable time.

Pubs and Cafés

Despite the stature of the cliffs in the gorge and the multitude of impressive climbs on offer to the public, Cheddar sees relatively few climbers and consequently has little in the way of a 'pub scene'. The main activists, mostly Bristol-based, generally retire to the warm comforts of city life for their evening's entertainment. The outside visitor, lacking a packed lunch and flask, can find daytime refreshment at the Caveman cafeteria, a large, soulless and expensive product of Cheddar's intensive tourist industry. An alternative during the summer months might be one of the multitude of over-priced 'ye olde' cream tea shops. Come the evening and opening time, things are not much better; while the crags themselves may be full of character and interest, the pubs are not. The Cliff Hotel, a free house, has a wide selection of good food at fairly reasonable prices, but an atmosphere as flat as the proverbial pancake. The Butchers Arms, a Courage pub just down the road, is slightly better – a selection of typical pub grub at standard prices, along with a pool table for those with the energy to spare.

The saving grace, pub-wise, stems from the location of Cheddar on the edge of the Mendip Hills, one of Britain's major caving areas. Two pubs, the Hunters Lodge and the Queen Victoria Inn, situated in the nearby village of Priddy, are the focal points for the caving community. With caving a second (usually winter) sport for many climbers in the region, they provide not only an excellent pint, but the best chance of some like-minded company.

Priddy is sited about 5 miles from Cheddar. Follow the road up the gorge (B3135), signposted to Bath and Wells, until a small staggered crossroads is reached. Turn right (the signpost indicates camping and caravans) and immediately a notice announces Priddy. Continue for nearly a mile and turn right just past Priddy Green for the Queen

Vic. The Hunters Lodge lies about 1½ miles past the green along the main road.

Both pubs will satisfy the needs of the discerning drinker, but choose the Queen Vic if food is a priority. The Hunters has a limited menu, but one admirably suited to the impecunious climber, while its spartan decor will readily accommodate the dirty or dishevelled.

Pubs

THE HUNTERS LODGE
PRIDDY
NR WELLS
SOMERSET
Telephone: (0749) 72275

Mine Hosts are Roger and Jackie Dors.

BEER
A free house.

FOOD
This is served at lunchtimes and evenings. The menu ranges from faggots and peas at £1.00, to chilli, bread and butter at £1.25. Hounds and beans is also offered (sounds a bit cruel to me).

FACILITIES
There is a games room with shove halfpenny, dominoes and cribbage. Dogs, children and muddy boots are allowed in the pub, but children are, correctly, restricted to the games room.

OPINION
Recommended in the *Good Beer Guide*, CAMRA.

QUEEN VICTORIA INN
PRIDDY
NR WELLS
SOMERSET BA5 3BA
Telephone: (0749) 76385

Mine Hosts are Geoff and Judy Baynes.

BEER
The pub is a free house.

| FOOD

Normal serving times. There is also a children's menu. Food available ranges from quiche and salad at £2.50, to breaded plaice with prawn and mushroom filling at £3.90. This can be followed down by morello cherry flan at £1.20. (One is already salivating freely . . .)

OPINION

Recommended in the *Good Beer Guide*, CAMRA.

The Wye Valley

MATT WARD

Pubs

THE RISING SUN (Recommended)
WOODCROFT
TIDENHAM
GLOUCESTERSHIRE
Telephone: (02912) 2470

Mine Hosts are Mr and Mrs L. A. Astbury. The village of Woodcroft is essentially a ribbon-type development along the B4228 road; the Rising Sun is an obvious feature of the village if climbing at Wintours Leap. If unfamiliar with the area, the best way of getting to the pub is to use the diagram on page 16 of the Wye Valley climbing guide (published by Cordee Leicester 1987). It is anticipated that a major civil engineering project (due for completion in December 1987) will have altered the course of the A48 road. The old A48 road (as marked) will probably be signposted Tutshill; take this, then continue as indicated on the diagram.

BEER
The Rising Sun is tied to Courage Breweries and the range of beers on sale includes Courage Best, Courage Dark Mild, Symonds Bitter and Hoffmeister Lager.

FOOD
Bar snacks are usually available, subject to the business of the pub, and up to about 9.00 p.m., but it is occasionally possible to purchase one after this time. The prices are very reasonable. Particularly recommended are the homemade steak and kidney pies. Vegetarian dishes are not specifically served, but sometimes salads of various kinds can be bought, and these would probably be the best bet.

FACILITIES
Immediately adjacent to the pub is Woodcroft Stores, a shop/post office where groceries, confectionery, tobacco, milk and other drinks are

available. It stays open until 6.00 p.m. (except for Wednesday – early closing day) and there is a public telephone just outside.

The Rising Sun has standard English licensing hours (11.00 a.m.–2.30 p.m. and 6.00 p.m.–11.00 p.m.). There is a well-used dart board but no other entertainments of this type. Overnight accommodation is available at the pub from time to time, but little other is available nearby in the village. A variety of diverse accommodation can be found in Chepstow (2 miles away) ranging from B&B to an assortment of hotels. The guide book gives the best directions to the nearest camp sites (page 8). The pub can become swamped with climbers, particularly during weekends and summer evenings, but is usually quiet with just a few regular locals. Permission to bring dogs or children into the pub should be sought and is at the discretion of the landlord, but failing this there is a pleasant sunny garden if conditions are suitable. Muddy boots seem to be tolerated, if not encouraged.

OPINION
The Rising Sun is a particularly popular drinking house for climbers and a friendly welcome is extended to climbers.

A climbers' new route book is kept behind the bar. This is particularly useful as it is the repository for the latest developments in the Wye Valley; it provides a source of up-to-date information for climbers visiting the area, and is the inspiration for much debate.

THE ROCK INN (Recommended)
HILLERSLAND
COLEFORD
GLOUCESTERSHIRE
Telephone: (0594) 32367

Mine Host is recently arrived Barry Allen. The Rock Inn is situated on the B4432 road, just a couple of miles north of Coleford. If approaching from the A40 Monmouth/Ross-on-Wye dual carriageway, this road is signposted first Symonds Yat East, then Coleford; the pub is 1 mile beyond Symonds Yat Rock itself.

BEER
This is a free house.

FOOD
There is an impressive selection of meals. These range from 'basket' type meals (chicken and chips, £1.80; 4 oz burger in bap, onions and chips, £1.75; plaice, chips and peas, £1.85; steak and kidney pie, chips and peas, £1.85 – all prices at October 1987) through to more substantial meals (salmon poached in white wine, £4.50; grilled sirloin steak 8 oz, £5.50; steak au poivre, £6.50). There are no vegetarian dishes

specifically prepared, but ploughman's lunches are available (cheddar ploughmans, £1.50; stilton ploughmans, £1.95).

FACILITIES

A large selection of beers is available for the connoisseur of real ales. The licensing hours are 11.00 a.m.–2.30 p.m. and 6.00 p.m.–11.00 p.m. There is a skittle alley, a games room, juke box and dart board. Also a telephone, on a long extension lead, kept behind the bar, which you have to ask for. The pub allows well-behaved dogs on the premises and children well behaved or otherwise, provided it is not very busy. Muddy boots are also acceptable. There is accommodation here; well-appointed rooms each with its own colour TV. For those seeking a little more economy (99.9 per cent of climbers!) there is limited camping, but unfortunately no facilities.

OPINION

Due to the proximity of the crags, the Rock Inn is convenient for climbers and is well used by a large number, the garden is a popular venue when the weather is good during the long summer evenings. There is a small new routes book (is this for small new routes?) for Symonds Yat and the Forest of Dean, kept behind the bar.

The Swanage Files

NIGEL COE

———◆———

'Sunday clears away the rust of the whole week.'

JOSEPH ADDISON

Swanage has an exceptionally mild climate, dries quickly, and boasts over 700 climbs spread over 5 miles of cliff. It is known for its steepness and the abundance of roofs but it also has a reputation for looseness. This reputation has less foundation nowadays for two reasons: new routes generally undergo thorough cleaning and the traffic on the popular longer-established routes has removed most of their loose rock. The Swanage guidebook is very informative on this aspect of the climbing. However, this reputation for looseness, together with the lesser predominance of climbing as a sport in the south means that here one can get away from the noise and the queues at other crags.

Recommended Cliffs for the Visitor

For a fleeting visit to Swanage, Subluminal or Guillemot Ledges are the best places to visit, as these cliffs are unaffected by nesting-season restrictions and are least dependent on sea conditions: Subluminal has a high starting ledge and Guillemot is barricaded from the sea by a jumble of huge boulders. Subluminal sports short (30-foot) solid lines between Diff and E3, whilst Guillemot has 100-foot routes varying between (hard!) Hard Severe and E5. The rock is less reliable than Subluminal but not too bad.

Disregard the instructions for entry into Guillemot given in the guidebook: since it went to press the ledge bearing the abseil stake felt the call of the wild – both ledge and stake (now bent through 90 degrees) are available for inspection 50 feet below. Abseil is now from a stake at the top of the descent gully.

For married climbers whose spouses and/or offspring fail to respond positively to the challenge of vertical severity, Swanage Bay's sandy beach is excellent for swimming and sandcastles. The coastal path is an alternative attraction and can be combined with exploring the long-abandoned quarries, searching for orchids or for the puffins that breed hereabouts.

Pubs and Cafés

The Durlston Castle is the best pub for climbers. The Square and Compass at Worth Matravers is an interesting stone-built pub. Unfortunately it is further away from the main climbing area and therefore of more interest to walkers, or climbers possessed by the urge to explore. Fortes (self-service restaurant open 9.00 a.m. to 5.30 p.m.) in Swanage High Street should only be used in dire emergencies, being expensive and characterless. A last resort on a rainy Sunday morning!

Pubs

DURLSTON CASTLE
LIGHTHOUSE ROAD
SWANAGE
DORSET BH19 7RJ
Telephone: (0929) 424693

Mine Hostess is Mrs Molloy. Directions to find Durlston Castle are: turn away from the seafront at the Victoria Hotel, up Seymer Road, left onto Durlston Road and continue along Lighthouse Road to the left-hand car park in the Durlston Country Park. The pub is down the slope amongst the trees.

BEER
The pub is a free house.

FOOD
Bar snacks are served on weekdays between 10.30 a.m. and 3.00 p.m. and between 6.00 p.m. and 11.00 p.m. On Sundays serving times are from 12.00 to 2.00 p.m. and from 7.00 p.m. to 10.30 p.m. Vegetarian dishes are offered. The menu contains a wide range of snacks, from salad sandwiches at 80p to crab salad at £3.75. Extra choice is offered depending on the season.

FACILITIES
There is a games room, pool table, juke box, dart board and public telephone, in fact the lot! And yes! dogs, children and boots are OK.

The pub is about five minutes from the crags and there is a new routes book behind the bar. Bunk accommodation is available, there are four rooms with between six and eight bunk spaces in each bedroom. The cost is £5 for bed plus coffee, or £6.50 for bed and breakfast, which is egg, bacon, sausage, fried bread and mushrooms.

COMMENT
Well, it sounds tailor-made for outdoor persons, doesn't it? The pub is popular with climbers and walkers and is recommended in the CAMRA guide. 'Worth a visit' say Wessex M.C.

THE SQUARE AND COMPASS
WORTH MATRAVERS
DORSET
Telephone: (0929 43) 229

BEER
The pub is tied to Whitbreads Brewery. Directions to find the pub are: take the A351 out of Swanage, turn left onto the B3069. After passing through Langton Matravers, turn left onto the road signposted Worth Matravers. The pub is on the right in the village. For car parking turn right; the car park is 50 yards on the left.

FOOD
No food is served.

FACILITIES
Children and muddy boots are allowed in.

COMMENT
The pub is recommended in CAMRA guide and although used by climbers, tends to be most popular with walkers.

Places to Stay

Camping

TOM'S FIELD CAMPING SITE
TOM'S FIELD ROAD
LANGTON MATRAVERS
NR SWANAGE
No phone number available.

Open Easter–30th September. Location: Approaching Swanage on A351, turn right onto B3069. At Langton Matravers turn left into Tom's Field Road, site at end of road.

PRIEST'S WAY HOLIDAY PARK
PRIEST'S WAY
SWANAGE
Telephone: Swanage 422747

Open 1st April–31st October. Location: Approaching Swanage on A351, 1 mile past 'Welcome to Swanage' sign take right-hand fork into high street, second right into Steer Road, then continue up the hill.

Cornwall
(including Devon and Dartmoor)

'Somewhere over the rainbow, skies are blue
And the dreams that you dare to dream
Really do come true

If happy little bluebirds fly beyond the rainbow
Why oh why can't I?'

ARLEN-HARBURG, AS SUNG BY MISS GARLAND
A good question Judy!

Cornwall

Perhaps the most surprising point about this lovely place is that it isn't a National Park; i.e. not a designated area of 'outstanding natural beauty'. Although it doesn't have the magnificence of Snowdonia or the Lakes, it is pretty; 'joy for the eyes'.

If you've never been to Cornwall, then save it for as long as possible to be able to look forward to something in this country. It's warm! A visit here is a real treat and should be treated as such. Make sure you take the obligatory holiday paraphernalia: bucket and spade, sun tan lotion and deck chairs. Climbing equipment is optional. There is so much more to do here than just climbing. There are tin mines to fall down, cream teas to bloat out on and a freezing cold Atlantic to dip your corns in. Keep to the bit around the edge (the technical term is *coast*) – you'll avoid the other punters and a quiet time will ensue.

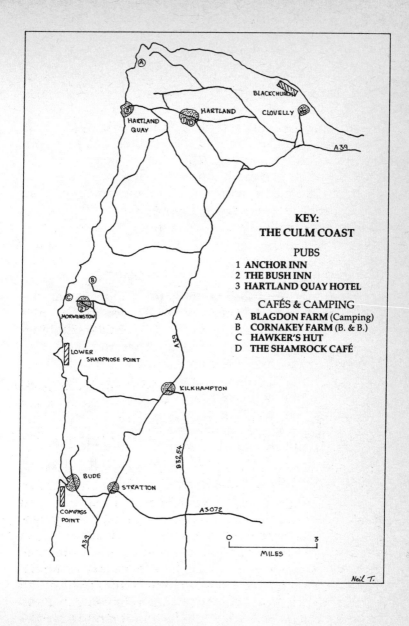

KEY:
THE CULM COAST

PUBS
1 ANCHOR INN
2 THE BUSH INN
3 HARTLAND QUAY HOTEL

CAFÉS & CAMPING
A BLAGDON FARM (Camping)
B CORNAKEY FARM (B. & B.)
C HAWKER'S HUT
D THE SHAMROCK CAFÉ

BLACKCHURCH
CLOVELLY
HARTLAND
HARTLAND QUAY
MORWENSTOW
LOWER SHARPNOSE POINT
KILKHAMPTON
BUDE
STRATTON
COMPASS POINT

A39
A3072
B3254

0   3
MILES

Neil T.

The Area

In Cornwall there are masses of fun things for the whole family, although nothing for single-parent families, sorry. The coastal footpath runs within gazing distance of the sea and small manageable sections are certainly worth doing, wandering up hill and down beach. The views vary from 'ooh!' to 'aah . . .'. The smart walker will aim to spend the afternoon rambling slowly over Sennen Beach, pausing for a bracing swim and a few hours' dozing in the sun, or maybe just wandering in an elderly fashion across the seemingly endless expanse of sand.

The Climbing

Climbing in Cornwall has long been a focus for the middle grade and family climber, indeed in the pre-Pembroke era, this was the 'in' place for Easter climbing, the rough Cornish granite and mild weather attracting climbers from all over the country; the M5, and then the A30, funnelling climbers' jumble wagons ever southwards. Everyone holidayed in Cornwall then. Nowadays it is fair to say that the area attracts the lower-grade climber seeking classic climbs and peace. However, local activists Roland and Mark Edwards have done their bit for the harder end of things, so there is something for everyone. The Edwards are resident at Compass West and are happy to supply information about routes in the area.

Devon

The Culm Coast

Where every repeat of a classic line can be a first ascent (please replace the holds after use). Actually, Culm's reputation for loose rock is a deliberate ploy put about by a small band of devotees who wish to keep to themselves

the excellent climbing and scenery of this 'forgotten' coastline.

Hartland
The little beach (when the tide's out) or the small museum of shipwrecks (when the tide's in) are useful distractions for the kids while Dad or Mum grabs a quick climb. When the weather permits, you can sit outside, pint in hand, and watch the antics on the one-pitch slabs of Screda Point ('Look, Mummy, real climbers!'). If the weather does not permit and you've already paid your money for the toll road and car park, then you can sit inside, stare at the photographs of local shipwrecks and contemplate the awful prospect of sea-level traverses along this coast (a perverse local sport best conducted on a rising tide at dusk).

The toll road (60p last summer) is free in winter, but then the pub might well be closed too – so phone to check.

Morwenstow and Cornakey
Strictly speaking, Morwenstow and Cornakey are in Cornwall (just), but they are a world away from Land's End and Bosigran, or even the tourist beach at Bude (6 miles to the south).

Pubs

THE ANCHOR INN
THE SQUARE
HARTLAND
Telephone: (02374) 414

The pub is at the eastern end of the town, on the corner of the Bude turning.

BEER
Bass.

FOOD
Usual pub grub – pasties, scampi and chips in a basket, etc.

FACILITIES
Large car park and two large bars. Children are allowed in the
'restaurant' bar. In the main bar there is a pool table and a dart board.

THE BUSH INN
MORWENSTOW
Telephone: (028883) 242

BEER
It is a free house selling real ale.

FOOD
Very good home-cooked food, but usually at dinnertimes only.

FACILITIES
A huge log fire.

THE FIRST AND LAST INN (Highly Recommended)
SENNEN
CHURCHTOWN
LANDS END
CORNWALL TR19 7AA
Telephone: (0736) 87 680

Mine Host is Mr Pete Smith. The pub is situated 1½ miles from Lands
End on the A30.

BEER
The pub is a free house.

FOOD
Bar snacks are served between 11.00 a.m. and 2.30 p.m. and between
6.00 p.m. and 11.00 p.m. Vegetarian dishes are available. There is a
wide range of food available.

FACILITIES
Provided for our delectation are a games room, pool table, juke box,
dart board and public telephone. Dogs, children and muddy boots are
OK.

OPINION
Probably the best pub in the area. The welcome is very friendly and the
mixture of locals and visitors makes for a lively atmosphere. The bar
staff all seem very jolly, if a touch eccentric; the first time I visited all
the bar ladies were dancing around in a devil-may-care fashion, and
the second time the landlord criticized my darts playing and mocked
my trousers. They do know how to have a good time down there!
Worth a visit.

THE GURNARDS HEAD HOTEL
ZENNOR
ST IVES
CORNWALL TR26 3DE
Telephone: (0736) 796928

Mine Hosts are Mr and Mrs J. J. Major. The pub is sited on the B3306 coast road 13 miles from Lands End.

BEER
The pub is a free house.

FOOD
Both bar snacks and restaurant food are served between the hours of 11.00 a.m. and 2.30 p.m. and then from 6.30 p.m. to 11.30 p.m. Vegetarians are not always guaranteed being pandered to.

FACILITIES
The only distraction here is a dart board. Dogs are not allowed in. Children are allowed in at the discretion of the landlord. Muddy boots within reason are acceptable. The pub is well used by climbers and walkers. It is the nearest to the Climbers Club hut, the Count House at Bosigran, and is handy for climbers returning from the Gurnards Head climbs.

OPINION
Gurnards Head is Cornish for 'Gurnards Head'.
  OK, but gloomy atmosphere at opening time was not alleviated by the 'cheerful' bar staff.

HARTLAND QUAY
HARTLAND
Telephone: (02374) 218

BEER
It is a free house, selling real ale.

FACILITIES
Pool table. Children and pets welcome. Within staggering distance of the beach and a short boulder hop to the nearest crag.

THE LANDS END PUB
STATE HOUSE
LANDS END
CORNWALL TR19 7AA
Telephone: (0736) 87 501

Mine Host is Mr Brian Whitta. The pub is situated at the end of the A30 overlooking the western approaches. You can't miss it really.

BEER
The pub is a free house.

FOOD
Both restaurant and bar snacks are served between the hours of 11.00 a.m. and 2.30 p.m. and 6.00 p.m. and 11.00 p.m. Vegetarian dishes are served and the menu is 'very comprehensive'.

FACILITIES
These include a games room, pool table, dart board and public telephone. Dogs, children and muddy boots are allowed in. The pub is reasonably well used by climbers and more so with walkers since it is very central to the Cornish coastal footpath.

OPINION
This pub is highly recommended between the hours of 7.00 p.m. and 8.30 p.m. You can watch the sunset and look out over the ocean, the Atlantic actually, and realize that the next piece of land is America. Gosh it makes you think, sat there with a pint in one hand gazing reflectively over the great expanse of greyness, watching the great red orb sinking, bleeding slowly into the West, just to the left of the flagpole near the postcard stand.

The pub is part of a complex of buildings catering for the passing trade of tourists; there are all manner of things for parting you from your money, ignore them, go to the bar, close your ears to the muzak, gaze not at the plush surroundings, merely buy some beer and get a good seat near the window. Better still sit outside and relax to enjoy an hour or so of ocean gazing.

THE LOGAN ROCK INN
TREEN
ST LEVAN
PENZANCE
CORNWALL TR19 6LG
Telephone: (0736) 810495

Mine Hosts are Peter and Anita George.

BEER
The pub is tied to the St Austell Brewery.

FOOD
Both bar snacks and restaurant food are served between 12.00 and 2.00 p.m., except Sundays when it is to 1.30 p.m. During the evening

177

serving times are 6.00 p.m. to 9.00 p.m. (June to September) and from 7.00 p.m. to 9.00 p.m. October to May. The menu ranges from sandwiches and baked potatoes at 75p to steaks at £6.00. The pub has two specials: the Logan Rock Seafarer and the Longships Bake, at £2.50 each.

FACILITIES
There is a games room, pool table, juke box and dart board. Dogs on leads are OK. Children are allowed in the children's room. Muddy boots are OK within reason. Local farms and camp sites supply accommodation. The pub is recommended in other guides and is popular with climbers and walkers.

THE PLUME OF FEATHERS
PRINCETOWN
DARTMOOR

COMMENT
'Highly recommended. Bunkhouse accommodation. Good food and also breakfasts served.'

THE PRINCE OF WALES HOTEL
PRINCETOWN
YELVERTON
DARTMOOR
Telephone: 219

Mine Hosts are Mr and Mrs Wallace.

BEER
The pub is a free house.

FOOD
Both bar snacks and restaurant food are served from 10.30 a.m. to 10.30 p.m. No vegetarian food.

FACILITIES
A dart board and B&B. Dogs, children and muddy boots are welcomed.

COMMENT
The Prince is recommended in good food and beer guides.

THE RADJAL (Worth a Visit)
PENDEEN
CORNWALL

'Radjal' is Cornish for 'fox'. This is a fairly traditional type of pub and popular with locals. A cheerful atmosphere is induced by the many pictures of local wrecks of the shipping sort; 'BUSBY wrecked at Pendeen 1896' captions a photograph of a half-sunk trawler . . . What about 'Gill, Bill & Johnson wrecked in Pendeen 1987'?

FACILITIES
These include a pool table, a juke box and cheerful atmosphere.

There are two other pubs in Pendeen which are sometimes frequented by climbers, the North and the Trevellard Arms.

The **North** is set back off the road and is less exciting than an ingrowing toenail.

The **Trevellard Arms** was recommended to me by Pat (Littlejohn). 'It's the only place to go,' he said. 'It is situated in the middle of Pendeen and is very hectic; lots of eye-catching techniques needed to get served. It is very handy for walking home if you're stopping at the camp site, Levnant House.'

THE SHIP INN
CHUDLEIGH
DEVON

COMMENT
The pub is on the main road through the town. South Devon M.C. meet here and say it is worth a visit. Their meeting times are on the second and fourth Wednesdays every month except August. From October to April the time is 8.00 p.m. and the rest of the year they meet at 9.00 p.m.

THE WELLINGTON
WELLINGTON STREET
NR NORTH HILL
PLYMOUTH
Telephone: (0752) 661133

'The Wellie' is on the corner of Wellington Street and Deptford Place, just off North Hill – a short walk from Plymouth Polytechnic.

BEER
Draught beer.

FOOD
Bar food served.

FACILITIES
No pets or children allowed.

COMMENT
The current weekly venue for Plymouth-based climbers. Popular with younger people and students.

THE WINE BAR
FORE STREET
TOTNES
DEVON

Found near the top of Fore Street on the left, 200 yards past the arch.

BEVERAGES
Wine and good draught beer.

FOOD
Excellent vegetarian and meat dishes.

FACILITIES
No children or pets, but you are likely to meet the occasional climber here.

THE WRECKERS
SENNEN
CORNWALL

COMMENT
This barn of a pub has a summer licence only and consequently smells a bit musty at the beginning of the season. However, they have a disco which goes on till late and if you fancy a knees up, this is the place. At least it isn't far to stagger back to the camp site.

Cafés

DART CAFÉ
THE PLAINS
TOTNES
DEVON

At the bottom of the hill, by the river.
   A good-value café, offering cups or mugs and good vegetarian or meat dishes, also cakes.

THE SHAMROCK CAFÉ
THE SQUARE
HARTLAND
Telephone: (02374) 243

Proprietress, Mrs O'Donnell. Approaching Hartland from the A39 from
Bideford or Bude, the Shamrock is on the main street on the left, just
before the square. A green shamrock and a fish are painted outside.
Park in the square.

The café is the back room of a small grocer's shop-cum-village store
which doubles as the local chippy in the evenings and as a newsagent
on Sundays. For gamblers, a one-penny one-armed bandit fruit
machine is squeezed in between the vegetables and the fish counter/
newspaper rack.

Mrs O'Donnell runs all these concerns and still finds time to brew a
pot of tea strong enough to stand a spoon in – visitors are well advised
to order extra boiling water. Food is typical English breakfast – beans,
cheese, sausage, etc., on toast or with chips. Top of the list of places to
stock up before a trying day on the superb extremes at Exmansworthy
or Blackchurch, or the less demanding, sunnier slabs around Hartland
Quay. A stop here for breakfast has the advantage that you can also
buy all your snacks and munchies for a day on the crag, as well as
obtain information as to camp sites, B&B, etc.

Places to Stay

CORNAKEY FARM
Telephone: Mrs Hayward (028883) 260

This offers excellent B&B and children are welcome. The best approach
for Gull Rock and Cornakey Cliff is from here – please park carefully
and ask at the farm.

Those more adventurous climbers, un-encumbered with children or
money, may wish to risk a bivouac. Scramble two-thirds of the way
down the vegetated spur to the NORTH of Cornakey Cliff (*not* south –
this is Wreckers' Slab, 400 feet, VS) and you may find a strange buried
shelter set on a slight shoulder. Initials scratched on the planks inside
bear witness to previous visits by impecunious climbers.

This look-out was actually built during the last war by the local air
and coast observer corps (God, they must have been bored!). It is in a
state of semi-collapse, but should shelter two or three huddled
climbers if wind and rain disturb the comfort of the flat grass
immediately outside.

HAWKER'S HUT
Just above VICARAGE CLIFF
MORWENSTOW

In similar vein to the above, with equally splendid views of sea and sea, this is a slightly larger construction of flotsam and timber, built by the Victorian vicar of Morwenstow to watch for shipwrecks. An uncomfortable bivi has been spent here.

LEVNANT HOUSE
PENDEEN

A pleasant, clean, reasonably quiet site.

RUDA PARK CARAVAN AND CAMPING SITE
BAGGY POINT

Baggy Point is a rightly popular climbing venue, although the delights and disco of the huge camping site at Croyde may wear off more quickly than your fingertips on Baggy's coarse sandstone slabs. There's no local alternative, so it's best to relax and enjoy it.

In the **SENNEN** area there is:

Sea View
This is OK if you like it noisy and just want to roll out of the pub into your tent.

Trevendra Farm
This is more a family site, quieter and further from the village.

Lower Treave Farm
This is quieter still and probably has the best facilities in the area.

SMOOTHLANDS
BLAGDON FARM
HARTLAND POINT

There are many regular camp sites in north Devon – this is not one of them. Facilities nil – but the situation is wonderful – impressive cliffs, hard and easy climbing within walking distance, a flat meadow in a sheltered valley to camp in, and plenty of driftwood on the beach for a camp fire.

You would be ill advised to drink from the small streams and waterfalls in these Culm Coast valleys – there's no telling what agricultural waste or farmyard slurry drains into their brown waters – but there's a tap in Hartland Village.

Other Points and Places of Interest in Cornwall

Pendeen bakery serves Cornish pasties, 18 oz and good fare. It opens early.

In Penwith/Newlyn town, there is a small shop selling homemade ice cream with clotted cream; it's delicious if a trifle fattening. In fact, why not slap it straight on your hips?

Newlyn town also has a couple of meaderys which are a good night out, assuming you like mead. Or try the one next to the Trewellard Arms in Pendeen.

COMPASS WEST (Recommended)
INTERNATIONAL SCHOOL OF ROCK-CLIMBING (Good name eh?)
SENNEN
NR LANDS END
CORNWALL
Telephone: (073687) 447

The I.S.R. is a centre run by Roland, Betty and Mark Edwards, offering a number of facilities apart from the usual in-house climbing, walking and canoeing courses.

FACILITIES
There is a café which is open for business most of the year and 'will provide sustenance to any climber who calls in, within reasonable hours that is'. Mainly breakfasts, snacks, pasties and cream teas. The atmosphere is very relaxed and friendly. There are many pictures of Mark Edwards climbing, decorating the walls. MHHmmm . . . The café probably seats about 22. One important point is that it is also licensed.

A small shop provides a small amount of climbing gear and guidebooks. This will hopefully be extended in the near future.

A small gym is available. Climbers who find themselves rained off (what! It never rains in Cornwall!) can come and use the pull-up bar and finger boards. Future plans are to increase this to a full mini gym with weights, etc. This facility will be open night and day, although a small charge will be made.

New route books for the area are also kept here and if you need information about the area, the Edwards are happy to give you the benefit of their extensive local knowledge.

The centre offers two types of accommodation. There is the climbing centre which is a step up from the usual bunkhouse-style doss. Also further up the accommodation ladder is the guest house which offers little luxuries like TV and single/double bedrooms.

Future plans include the erection of an indoor climbing wall in 1988–89, which will be available at a small charge.

OPINION
Worth a visit if you're in the area. There are no 'climbers' cafés' and the centre provides a friendly welcome and pleasant surroundings for visiting climbers and walkers.

The South East

Oh, where to start! What a wonderful opportunity to
further damage North–South relations; the us and them
syndrome which seems set to divide this once united
country of ours! In the allocation of resources climbing
must be one of the few areas where God was feeling
generous, distributing the crags and rocky places with an
unfairness I wholly applaud. Who needs employment
when The Peak District, The Yorkshire Dales and The
Lakes are on the doorstep? OK for us up north but all out
of easy reach for the active Southern climber. Small
wonder then that those climbing areas that do exist in the
South, are guarded and cherished. Bowles Rocks, near
Tunbridge Wells, for instance is lovingly cared for and
protected against harmful influences like chalk and broad
Northern accents whilst the outdoor centre here is all
things to all men, with a variety of activities happening.
Not only climbing but a dry ski slope, an assault course, a
swimming pool, canoeing and so on. A good use of space
and resources; a thoroughly modern multi-functional
crag. Well done!

However despite, or maybe because of, the lack of
cragging facilities the area is well served with climbing
walls and clubs serving as focal points for social gatherings. In London particularly there are hundreds of activities to partake of between climbing sessions.

185

Bowles Rock, South East England

I had a taste of what goes on down South recently. Visiting friends I was woken on Sunday morning by a call; 'Do you want to go to see a fight?' asked the caller. 'Er, I'm not sure, who's fighting?' thinking in terms of Bomber Graham or maybe Mike Tyson. 'Mick and Victor!' came the reply. I'm not too well up with the boxing world and didn't recognize the names as world champions. I prevaricated, 'Er, well I'm not sure . . .' 'No, no' said my pal, 'It's Mick Fowler and Vic Saunders!' 'Crikey' I said. 'You mean Mick Fowler and Victor Saunders, two of Britain's most talented, brave courageous and bold mountaineers?' 'Er, well sort of . . . yes . . . it must be the same pair I suppose, they do climb a bit.' 'Great!' I thought. I like a good grudge match before dinner.

The fight took place in a pub in the East End at Sunday lunchtime, watched by scores of baying Cockneys and was organized, refereed and properly executed. It turned out not to be a grudge match but a bit of sport and is popular East End entertainment, along with the lady who stepped into the ring without a vest on. Not a pretty sight.

As for the outcome of the fight? It would be grossly unfair of me to say who won, but it wasn't Victor.

Dover

Apparently there is climbing at Dover. It seems pretty daft to me. Climbing at Dover! But what do I know about sea-cliff climbing with ice-axes, crampons and advanced rope techniques? In fact, what does anyone know about it? There is one person who knows about it and Mick Fowler has taken time out from bashing his mates to kindly give me the benefit of his experience. He has reported all information given on Dover. (Thank you, Mick.)

Southern Sandstone   *by Dave Turner*

Southern sandstone is extremely popular with climbers in the South East, so much so, that the main crags, Bowles and Harrisons, frequently resemble the popular end of Stanage; very crowded and good venues for posing. However away from these two areas there are hardly any climbers at all and solitude, if that's your scene, is readily found. High Rocks, Eridge Green, Under Rocks and Bulls Hollow area are all good venues, particularly for those climbing 5c and higher. As a whole the area is unusual because of its pleasant 'England our England' woodland settings, contrasting greatly with the bleakness of many Northern crags. Furthermore, because of the soft nature of the rock, there is a local toproping ethic, which makes the area a very relaxed playground, with no thoughts of 'mind blowing runnouts on impending headwalls' etc. Laid back is the general attitude down here.

There are numerous pubs in the area of which the Crown Inn at Groombridge is perhaps currently the most popular with local climbers. Other pubs worth visiting are The Boars Head Freehouse, on the A26 between Tunbridge Wells and Crowborough about a mile towards the latter from Eridge Station, and also the Huntsman Inn next to Eridge Station.

There is also a café in Groombridge – The Kandy Kaff – run by the local tycoon who also runs a Kandy Shop, a Kandy Kars taxi and mini bus service and a Kandy video shop – look out for the KKK. The Kaff used to be Terry's Festerhaunt, run by Terry Tullis and the late Julie Tullis. It is very cheap and good value for money, with a pleasant atmosphere, though the service is not up to Boris Becker speeds. There is a new routes book here as well, which deserves more attention, i.e. a bit more mindless abuse etc.

Pubs

THE ALBION
DOVER

This pub is in central Dover and is well spoken of and has been known to be pleasantly low in standard.

THE COASTGUARD PUB
DOVER

This is sited on the sea front at St Margarets Bay and is the nearest pub to the cliffs. It is OK, although not as good as the others.

THE CROWN INN
GROOMBRIDGE VILLAGE GREEN
KENT
Telephone: (089 276) 742

Mine Host is Mr Rhodes.

BEER
The Crown is a free house.

FOOD
Restaurant food is served in the evenings only, except Sunday. Bar snacks are served from 12.00 to 2.00 p.m. and between 6.00 p.m. and 10.00 p.m. Vegetarians are catered for.

FACILITIES
Children are allowed in the children's room. Dogs are allowed in. No muddy boots. A public telephone is on hand. B&B is available from £25.

COMMENTS
'Good beer, great food, friendly but a bit plummy.'
   'Good food and beer but often packed with grockles – worth a visit.'

THE HUNTSMAN INN
ERIDGE STATION
EAST SUSSEX TN3 9LE
Telephone: (089 276) 258

Mine Host is B. G. Bailey and the pub is on the main Tunbridge Wells to Crowborough road (A26) at Eridge Railway Station.

BEER
The Huntsman is tied to King & Barnes.

FOOD
Bar snacks are served from 12.00 to 2.00 p.m. at dinnertime and from 7.00 p.m. to 9.15 p.m. in the evening. No veggie stuff. Sandwiches and hot dogs are in the 60–80p range and meals are priced between £1.30–£2.50. Now that seems very reasonable to me.

FACILITIES
Bar billiards table, juke box and dart board are on hand for amusement. Dogs and children (not babies, thank goodness) are given the thumbs up. Muddy boots are OK so long as it's clean mud! (What can this mean!)

The pub is close to Bowles Outdoor Pursuit centre.

COMMENTS
'Excellent beer, good food, the owner encourages climbers in!! First choice – highly recommended!'

And 'Good food and friendly landlord.'

NB: none of these comments were made by people called Bailey.

The pub is also recommended in the *Good Beer Guide* and is popular with climbers and walkers.

THE WHITE HORSE INN
DOVER

Mine Host is Charles Willett and the pub is sited about half a mile from the ferry terminal.

FOOD
Food is served in the form of bar snacks, between the hours of 12.00 and 2.00 p.m. and from 6.30 p.m. to 9.30 p.m. On Sundays serving times are from 12.00 to 1.30 p.m. and from 7.30 p.m. to 9.30 p.m. On Thursdays only toasted sandwiches are available. Food on offer varies from soup and roll at 80p, to beef goulash and rice at £2.00.

FACILITIES
There is a pool table.

COMMENT
The food is OK. The pub is occasionally visited by climbers. The landlord does not complain when one sits in the corner all night leaving very impressive chalk stains. ('Oh Mick! What have you been up to?')

Cafés

Mick says, 'There are two rather cuddly fishermen's cafés which open at 7.00 a.m. on Sundays. They are close together on the main sea front road and reached as follows: from Dover Ferry terminal take the sea front road running east to the first roundabout (about 1 mile); continue on the sea front road for a quarter of a mile to two cafés on the right. The first one, the **Goya Café**, is probably the best and is run by two old dears, as all the best cafés are. There are lots of fishermen, but not many climbers.

The South East Appendix

THE BLACK LION
BRIGHTON ROAD
SURBITON
SURREY

Surbiton and Kingston M.C. meet here about 9.30 p.m. on Thursdays.

THE BULLS HEAD
TUNBRIDGE WELLS

COMMENT
'Worth a visit.'

THE FALKLANDS ARMS
BLOOMSBURY WAY
LONDON WC1

This pub is sited on the corner of Bloomsbury Way and Bury Street.
    The Rockhoppers M.C. meet here on the first and third Wednesday of each month at 8.00 p.m.

FAT HARRY'S
BERRIMAN ROAD
LONDON N7

The Ibex Club take refreshments here after visiting the Sobell Wall. Rated 'OK'.

THE HORSE AND CROWN
MERATORIA
ST LEONARDS ON SEA
SUSSEX

Hastings Rock and Fell Club meet here on the third Tuesday of each month at 8.00 p.m.

THE MASONS ARMS
ST MARYS LANE
UPMINSTER
ESSEX

The South Essex C.C. meet here on the first Friday of each month at 9.00 p.m.

THE OLYMPIC BAR
LUTON REGIONAL SPORTS CENTRE
STOPSLEY
LUTON

The BEDROC (Bedfordshire Rock Outdoor & Cave Club) meet here after a session on the wall from 10.00 p.m. until kicking out time.

THE PEACOCK
MAIDEN LANE
COVENT GARDEN
LONDON WC1

The Ibex Club meet here on the first Wednesday of each month at 8.00 p.m. until closing time.

THE SHIP
47 HIGH STREET
CROYDON

Croydon M.C. meet here on the first and third Wednesday of each month at 8.30 p.m.

Climbing Walls

'Action is the last resort of those who know not how to dream.'

OSCAR WILDE

The Development of the Climbing Wall and its Influence on the Sport of Rock Climbing

Since the inception of the climbing wall concept at Leeds University in the 1960s, the wall scene has evolved into a sport far removed from a merely supportive role in the training schedule of the dedicated rock athlete. A visit to one of the more popular walls highlights the fact that it is now a game as far removed from traditional rock climbing as that sport is distant from mountaineering. Whilst it may now seem strange that rock climbing was once regarded as merely a training aid for the 'greater' challenges of the Alps and the Himalayas, I can still remember days spent at Stanage as a wobbly beginner, hearing some hard mountaineering type (baggy breeches, shaggy beard and sagging belly), refer dismissively to that glorious adventure playground as 'not the real thing', i.e. not a proper mountain, which any twit could see.

The poor man excused his demise on a VS with, 'Of course, I don't really function below 18,000.' I felt sorry for his wife.

Today's wall-freaks, technically known as WALL-EES, are easily recognized by their demeanour and garb; forearms like whipped steel; torsos rippling; sinewy and completely hip-less,* whilst earrings and prize-winning hair arrangements are *de rigueur* almost to the point of (dare I say it? yes, yes I dare! I dare!) . . . conformity.

Gymnastically superb, the wall buff encounters occasional difficulties in the transference of skills to the outdoor situation: 'Bye 'eck, he can't climb sod all but you should see 'im at Dickie's . . . he can do this one finger dyno from a two thumb pinch undercut . . . and the amazing thing is he's never more than six inches from the deck, the main problem is stopping yer bum scraping the floor . . .'

Despite this minor problem of application, the value of the climbing wall is well recognized. Apart from the hordes of neckless whippets the walls have spawned, there has also been the odd star; the example of Yorkshire's John Dunne springs to mind. Once known affectionately behind his back as Porky, he is now the Human Wedge since training hard. However, he has paid the price and hasn't written anything decent since that very stirring piece about seconding. 'Never send to know for whom the rope pulls. It pulls for thee.'

With over 250 walls in this country, almost everyone has access to this now well-established training tool. Except me. I'd like to take this opportunity to point out that Buxton climbing wall is currently falling down and I'd like to know what's being done about it . . . I know it's not much, but it was good enough for Simon Nadin and that's good enough for me . . . well, I've said my piece now so you know how I feel . . . right, where was I . . . Oh yes, back to the wall . . . (the story of my life . . .)

The Climbing Wall: the Use Thereof

One of the major attractions of the walls, particularly in the British autumn and winter (OK and the spring and

*i.e. without hips, not without fashion.

Climbing Walls

summer) is the opportunity to integrate with others of a similar ilk, or failing that, other climbers. There is bound to be some extra-mural socializing afterwards (the correct term is a SESSION) and useful contacts can be established for weekend sessions.

The best times for visiting walls are midweek evenings or rainy weekends, as they will be completely packed out, making physical communion between you and the wall of your choice an impossibility, leaving more time for making friends (A PICK UP), and climbing chatter (BULLSHITTING).

1 To get you started, here are a few suggestions for opening lines:

'Ooh, Gavin I do like your tights, are they Beal or Pineapple Dance Studio?'

'Ooh, Jeremy, the nose stud! it's so "you"! What's that? No! Really! You did it yourself to impress a girl at a party? What? At the party? That's crucial!'

'Eh up Derek, you've split yer keks, ha ha!'

Variations on a theme could refer to earrings, hair styles, underpants, or pimples.

A note of warning. Once you have selected a buddy (look for bright alert eyes, willing disposition and a wet nose), it will take some time to forge a solid working relationship. Questions about whose round it is, or whose turn it is to drive home from the pub will arise, but with a little patience and a carefully planned training programme, you will soon have a well-motivated cheerful pet, er, I mean climbing partner. You might even get some good routes done. Ding, Dong. Do I hear wedding bells?

2 Working up a sweat. (Not to be confused with Exercise.) Watching all those rising, and falling, stars performing all that tricky body manoeuvering certainly makes the palms perspire.

'Will he fall off? . . . Will she make that move? . . . Will they crash in flight? . . . Have they . . . ?'

A gentle trickle will slip surely down the small of your back. Damp patches will form under your armpits and pretty soon you'll be dripping in all the right places. This is the Macho 6b Leader Sopping Wet Look. You'll smell awful but look great.

3 Trend Spotting

This is like bird spotting, but easier since trends in the climbing world are blatantly obvious.

It is important to spot the latest trends. Just think how absolutely awful it would be to arrive at the crag clad in gold lamé during the striped period. The shame of it! Unthinkable! No, it is far better to keep a watchful eye, by regular attendance at the wall, on the current fashions. By attentive monitoring of the spasms of the moment, you could get a name for yourself.

4 Practising Moves

The safety of the artificial climbing wall is the perfect environment for practising moves. Having perfected the various techniques necessary before 'coming out', the articulate wall rat will be able to put on a good show on the rock, or at least fairly close to it.

Some moves to think about are:

Tight Changing

This is an artform in itself. How to reveal enough knicker leg to tantalize but not shock? It's a tricky one this and needs some thought, particularly at those places prone to public attention, such as Malham Cove in Yorkshire or Raven Tor in Derbyshire. Pay attention to undergarments as 'tatty' equates with 'mucky' in the 'Shock A Granny' stakes.

Falling off and Landing Gracefully

One should not 'fall off' so much as 'float down'. Grace
and dignity at all times. Practise smiling serenely as you
fly through the air. It is uncool to scream unless you think
you are actually going to die, and then, by jove, you'd
better make sure you sustain some interesting injuries
because people have a nasty habit of remembering the
time you shattered glass in the pursuit of a sprained
ankle.

To lessen the impact of bone on concrete, try bend-
ing the knees on landing. Crashing head-first? You've
blown it.

Boots

Rock boots have to be laced tight because of the pain. I
don't know why pain is so important, but there you go, it
is, so you might as well accept it. This could be the reason
why so many climbers have trouble walking – it's called
hobbling. You can actually tell the grade a person climbs
at by the way they walk. People leading below E1 walk
perfectly normally because their boots are so floppy and
comfortable. Between the grades of E1 and E4 climbers
hobble because of the boot tightness. From E5 upwards
there is a tendency to hobble and mince . . .

Techniques

There are moves and techniques too numerous to mention. What about chalk bag dipping? Nail clipping? Hair
brushing? Contract signing? And so it goes on.

Practising the basics will give you an advantage. It's a
big world and as Clint once said, 'A man's got to have an
edge.' Then he shot a few people.

5 Personal Hygiene

Many of today's ultra modern high tec sports centres have
washing facilities or, if it's Yorkshire, a communal sink.

6 Sneaking a Look

Thanks to the invention of the wide bridging move, you can sometimes look up men's shorts. Don't do this unless (a) you want to pick up that person, or (b) want a punch in the teeth.

The Climbing Wall: Construction of

Climbing walls come in several shapes and sizes, ranging from the purpose-built mini crag, such as the Ackers Trust in Birmingham, outside and massive, to scraped brick edges in a corridor. Most walls are situated in sports centres or educational establishments. Sports centre walls are often incorporated into the existing structure of the building. This can lead to the occasional overlapping of sporting interests. The badminton court makes an uneasy neighbour. (They don't like chalk on the courts, do they? My goodness that makes them slip about a bit!) This process of distraction works both ways though. Have you noticed how popular the wall becomes on a Wednesday afternoon? It's got nothing whatsoever to do with the ladies' aerobics classes. Oh no. In all fairness, I must say that some climbers are there to participate. It seems that aerobics and jazz dance classes are gaining popularity as training with certain climbers. Whilst I am the last person to point a finger, the prospect of a 15-stone Berzins pretending to be a willow tree blowing in a light breeze, or strutting his funky stuff to the pounding rhythms of Prince, is disconcerting. What if he trod on one of the little ones?

The construction of the wall is not just a matter of scratching out mortar from between bricks. (Actually the Buxton climbing wall was a forerunner of this technique which is probably why it's falling down.) People who 'know' design things, test them and do research just so that you and I can fall off in the winter as well. The wall

Climbing Walls – uses of 'sneaking a look'

construction business supports at least two specialist firms, the best known being Bendcrete and D.R. Climbing Walls Ltd which is the partnership of Don Robinson and Graham 'Streaky Bacon' Desroy, so-called because of his peculiar habit with rashers.

Some walls have faithfully reproduced crag features, such as chimneys, roofs and slabs; the more far-sighted offer cold draughts, slimy wet patches and queuing. Cunningly placed jutting rocks duplicate those chin-smashing falls as you hurtle downwards. (Why do you and I hurtle downwards, not upwards like the top rock stars do?)

Landing is important. Some walls thoughtfully provide crash mats for tripping over. Others prefer the no-nonsense approach; no soppy landing mattresses to wimp out on, just good old concrete to splatt on. Oh, the unforgettable crunch of bone on concrete!

Apart from the specific climbing facilities available at the centres, other interesting sporting activities are on offer. Weight training is usually close by but, considering how many hunky men get pumped up, it's an incredibly boring sport. The Richard Dunn Sports Centre in Bradford has a water sports area known as Splashland. I am reliably informed that the extensive water chutes can be exhilarating.

All in all, climbing walls are a GOOD IDEA and I wish I'd got a few bob behind certain people. Oh well, Tel Aviv as they say in Israel . . .

Climbing Wall Restrictions

Most walls operate restrictions of one sort or another for two reasons. One is to protect inexperienced climbers from hurting themselves. The second reason is to protect themselves against being held liable for any injuries sustained.

The rules vary from 'no chipping new holds', to signing indemnity forms. Some places require climbers to wear helmets, to stay below a certain height when soloing, to have competent climbers present, not to use chalk, and so on. Whilst certain rules seem petty and pointless, others are based on sound reason.

If you don't wear your helmet at the wall, just when are you going to get chance to wear it? Nobody wears a helmet on the crags, so you'll never get your money's worth if you don't use it at the wall.

Other rules strike me as odd. The height restriction is one. Some walls paint a line to indicate 'no go' areas for soloing, usually at about 15 feet. I think this is daft. Nobody in their right mind would solo above 15 feet anyway. The line should be drawn at about 6 or 7 feet, which would be more sensible. That's where my line is.

As time progresses, there will doubtless be more rules and controls. There may one day be a standard set of guidelines. Would it be possible to incorporate the following sensible ones?

1   No showing off. Don't you get sick of being burnt off by the local stars. I do.
2   No smelly feet or deliberately excessive sweating.
3   No standing around in cliques being disdainful of lesser climbers' attempts, pathetic though they are.
4   Don't say 'this is the first time I've ever looked at this problem, honestly' before flashing it first time.

However, if you think there are already too many 'do's and don'ts', you can always try an alternative plan for getting fit – go to a crag and do some climbing. It's worth a try.

Index of Climbing Walls

North West

LCOP CLIMBING WALL (Very Good)
c/o The Director (Colin Mortlock), Centre for Outdoor Education
CHARLOTTE MASON COLLEGE
AMBLESIDE
CUMBRIA LA22 9BB
Telephone: (0906) 33066. This is the college reception.

The climbing wall is open to the general public, and is found by following signs from the foot of the Kirkstone Pass road out of Ambleside along Nook Lane, or through the college campus *by foot* only, as cars are not allowed at the wall.

OPENING TIMES
These are from 8.30 a.m. to 9.45 p.m.

PRICE
The entrance fee is 70p per day or £15 for an annual season ticket.

RESTRICTIONS
Juniors must be supervised.

THE WALL
Self-contained designed and constructed by local climbers in 1984. Constructed from various materials. (Sounds a bit slapdash doesn't it?, but it's great.)
   The nearest major climbing area is the Lake District.

OTHER FACILITIES
A sports hall complex and further climbing facilities are due to be built in 1988 on the site adjacent to the climbing wall.

BOLTON METROPOLITAN COLLEGE (Worth a Visit if Convenient)
SPORTS HALL
MANCHESTER ROAD CENTRE
BOLTON BL2 1ER
Telephone: (0204) 31411 ext 3461

The wall is open to the general public on Thursdays between 7.00 p.m. and 9.00 p.m. and is situated off Manchester Road opposite W. H. Smiths 'Do-it-all' Superstore.

OPENING TIMES
As above during college term times. In 1988 this is 7/1/88 to 24/3/88 inclusive and 14/4/88 to 28/4/88 inclusive.

PRICE
The entrance fee is £1.00 per session.

RESTRICTIONS
None.

THE WALL
Incorporated into the sports hall walls and made from brick, concrete and wood attachments, built in 1971. It was designed by members of the local climbing fraternity.
   The nearest climbing areas are the Wilton Quarries and Brownstones.

OTHER FACILITIES
Weight training, shower and changing facilities are available.

THE SANDS CENTRE (Very Good)
THE SANDS
CARLISLE CA1 1JQ
Telephone: (0228) 25222

The climbing wall is open to the general public and is found by proceeding to Hardwick Circus roundabout, the main island in Carlisle. The centre is beside the island.

OPENING TIMES
Seven days a week between the hours of 10.00 a.m. and 10.00 p.m.

PRICE
The entrance fee is 85p, and 50p for juniors.

RESTRICTIONS
The only restriction is that under-sixteens must be supervised.

THE WALL
Incorporated into one end of a sports hall and made from bricks and blocks. Built in 1984 by Don Robinson.
   The nearest major climbing area is the Lake District.

OTHER FACILITIES
There are showers, changing and weight training facilities available. Also refreshments.

PELHAM HOUSE (Worth a Visit)
CAULDER BRIDGE
EGREMONT
CUMBRIA
Telephone: (0946) 84 234

OPENING TIMES
Access is restricted so ring to check availability.

PRICE
A nominal fee is charged.

THE WALL
Built in 1980 by climbers.

ELLESMERE PORT INDOOR CENTRE (E.P.I.C.) (Worth a Visit)
McGARVA WAY
ELLESMERE PORT
SOUTH WIRRAL
Telephone: (051) 355 6432

The wall is open to all and is sited on the corner of Stanny Lane and McGarva Way.

OPENING TIMES
The centre is open from 9.00 a.m. to 11.00 p.m. but the wall is subject to other sporting impingements so ring to check.

PRICE
Members pay 80p and non-members pay £1.10.

THE WALL
Built by climbers in 1984.

FACILITIES
All the usual ones plus a good bar.

LIVERPOOL UNIVERSITY P.E. DEPT (Worth a Visit)
LIVERPOOL L69
Telephone: (051) 709 6022

OPENING TIMES
The wall is open to staff and students of the university between the following times: Weekdays from 8.30 a.m. to 9.30 p.m. Saturdays from 8.30 a.m. to 3.00 p.m. Sundays from 10.00 a.m. to noon.

PRICE
Free.

THE WALL
Built on a raised wall in the sports hall. First constructed in 1966 and the low traverse wall was doctored by Bendcrete at the end of 1987 with the concrete drying in 1988.

MACCLESFIELD LEISURE CENTRE
PRIORY LANE
MACCLESFIELD
CHESHIRE
Telephone: (0625) 615602

The climbing wall is open to the general public and is found by following signs from the town centre.

OPENING TIMES
Between 9.30 a.m. and 9.30 p.m. Closed Saturday evenings during August.

PRICE
The entrance fee is 60p and discounts are offered to unemployed

people on Mondays, Wednesdays and Fridays between 10.00 a.m. and 12.00 at 30p.

RESTRICTIONS
Under-eighteens must be supervised.

THE WALL
Self-contained, made from bricks and concrete in 1981.
The nearest good crags are in the Peak District.

FACILITIES
All necessary facilities, such as weight training, showers, refreshments are available.

THE ABRAHAM MOSS LEISURE CENTRE (Very Good)
CRESCENT ROAD
CRUMPSALL
MANCHESTER M8 6UH
Telephone: (061) 795 7277 or 740 1491 ext 347

The climbing wall is open to the general public, subject to the restrictions below.

OPENING TIMES
At weekends between 9.00 a.m. and 5.00 p.m. During the week between 9.00 a.m. and 10.00 p.m., excluding Tuesday when the wall isn't available in the evening. Daytime use of the wall is subject to use by schools and colleges.

PRICE
The entrance fee is 45p. Discounts are available to holders of the Manchester resident leisure pass which grants free use between 9.00 a.m. and 12.00 on weekdays and between 12.00 to 5 p.m. at a reduced fee of 30p. At weekends after 5.00 p.m., use costs 30p.

RESTRICTIONS
School groups and juniors must be supervised.

THE WALL
Incorporated into one end of the sports hall and made from natural rock and brick. It was built in 1974 with further improvements being carried out in 1984 by Don Robinson.
The nearest major climbing area is the Peak District.

OTHER FACILITIES
These include shower and changing facilities and refreshments.

ALTRINCHAM SPORTS CENTRE (Very Good)
OAKFIELD ROAD
ALTRINCHAM
CHESHIRE WA15 8EW
Telephone: (061) 928 2217

The wall is open to everyone.

OPENING TIMES
From 9.00 a.m. to 11.00 p.m. throughout the week.

PRICE
The fee for use is 85p.

RESTRICTIONS
No juniors under twelve years old admitted. Between twelve and fourteen years old, people must be accompanied by an experienced adult climber.

THE WALL
The wall is made using multivarious rock in grand blocks. It was built in 1982 and designed by Dave Pearce and other local climbers.

FACILITIES
There are weight training facilities available, also a bar and café for refreshments.

THE ARMITAGE CENTRE (Very Good)
MANCHESTER UNIVERSITY
MANCHESTER
Telephone: (061) 224 0404

The wall is open to the general public and is sited in the Fallowfield area off Wilmslow Road behind Owen Park.

OPENING TIMES
From 12.00 to 11.00 p.m. every day.

PRICE
£1.00 for non students and 80p otherwise.

THE WALL
Built by Bendcrete Climbing Walls in 1987 of very simple design but effective. Rock injection into brickwork design.

FACILITIES
Usual sports centre facilities available.

SID'S SPORTS HALL (Worth a Visit)
STALYBRIDGE
NR MANCHESTER
Telephone: (061) 338 3528

The wall is open to everyone.

OPENING TIMES
Open Monday, Tuesday, Thursday from 12.00 to 4.30 p.m., Wednesday, Friday, Saturday, Sunday 12.00 to midnight.

PRICE
The entrance fee is £1.50.

RESTRICTIONS
None.

FACILITIES
There are showers and changing rooms. Refreshments are available.

North East

THE RICHARD DUNN SPORTS CENTRE (Very Good)
ROOLEY AVENUE
ODSAL
BRADFORD
WEST YORKSHIRE BD6 1EZ
Telephone: (0274) 307822

The climbing wall is open to the general public and is well signposted on leaving the M606 motorway into Bradford.

OPENING TIMES
Between 9.00 a.m. and 7.00 p.m. on Saturdays, 9.00 a.m. to 9.00 p.m. on Sundays and 9.00 a.m. to 10.00 p.m. on weekdays.

PRICE
The entrance fee is £1.10 which includes 25p admission to the centre. Discounts are available for groups with a leader, booking in advance at £5.20.

RESTRICTIONS
Climbers under eighteen years must be accompanied by an experienced leader.

THE WALL
Purpose-built incorporating a weight-training room. It is made from natural rock, breeze block (part simulated) and concrete, built in 1978 and designed by Don Robinson.
 The major climbing areas closest to the wall are the Yorkshire Dales, with Shipley Glen at Baildon and Caley at Otley.

FACILITIES
All the expected facilites are available.

UNIVERSITY OF BRADFORD SPORTS CENTRE
(Worth a Visit if Convenient but see restrictions)
GT HORTON ROAD
BRADFORD
WEST YORKSHIRE BD7 1DP
Telephone: (0274) 733466 ext 8474

The wall is open to the general public in university vacations and is situated on the main Great Horton road.

OPENING TIMES
Weekdays between the hours of 8.15 a.m. to 10.00 p.m., and at weekends between 9.00 a.m. to 5.00 p.m.

PRICE
The fee is 55p and discounts are available through a Public User Card system (1,000 are available) with which entry is 45p.

RESTRICTIONS
No individual use is allowed (!)

THE WALL
Built at one end of a sports hall, made from concrete brick and stone, built in 1973 and designed by Mr Frank Murray, a former director of recreation.
    The nearest major climbing area is the Yorkshire Dales.

OTHER FACILITIES
All facilities, such as weight training, shower and changing, and refreshments are at hand.

THE LINDSEY CLIMBING WALL (Worth a Visit)
LINDSEY CLIMBING CLUB (c/o Pete Pounds)
GRAINSBY AVENUE
CLEETHORPES
SOUTH HUMBERSIDE DN35 9NX
Telephone: (0472) 694835

The wall is not open to the public. To use the wall you must join the club. It is found by taking the A180 to Cleethorpes. Halton Place school entrance is off Sandringham Road. The wall is in the Lindsey school gym.

OPENING TIMES
During term time, club members can use the wall on Thursdays between 7.00 p.m. and 9.00 p.m.

PRICE
The fee is 50p with discounts for under-eighteens and UB40s. They pay 30p.

RESTRICTIONS
Only supervised climbing is allowed.

THE WALL
One end of the sports hall, and made from brick and real rock. It was designed by Don Robinson and Graham Desroy and opened in 1984.
   The nearest climbing areas are the Derwent Valley, Stanage, etc.

FACILITIES
There are changing rooms and showers.

THE DOLPHIN CENTRE (Very Good)
HORSEMARKET
DARLINGTON
CO. DURHAM DL1 5QU
Telephone: (0325) 380 786

The climbing wall is open to the general public and is well signposted from the town.

OPENING TIMES
These are 9.00 a.m. to 10.00 p.m.

PRICE
The entrance fee is £1.00 for adults and 50p for children; 40p for school use. Discounts are available with a Leisuresaver pass, and 50 per cent reduction for UB40 holders.

RESTRICTIONS
There is an authorized user system in operation with recommendations for the use of helmets and supervised climbing for under-eighteens.

THE WALL
Occupies an original lift shaft used to bring heavy equipment into the sports hall and is made from brick, stone and concrete, built in 1982 and designed by (who else?) Don Robinson!
   The nearest crags are at Redcar, Eston Nab and Teesdale.

OTHER FACILITIES
Weight training, shower and changing, and refreshment facilities are available.

AIREBOROUGH LEISURE CENTRE (Very Good)
THE GREEN
GUISELEY
LEEDS LS20 9BT
Telephone: (0943) 77131

The wall is open to the general public and is found by following the A65 (Skipton/Leeds road) to Guiseley.

OPENING TIMES
At weekends from 8.00 a.m. to 10.30 p.m. and on weekdays from 9.00 a.m. to 10.30 p.m.

PRICE
Peak rates are operative at weekends and between 5.00 p.m. to 10.30 p.m. during the week. They are £1.25 for adults and 75p for juniors. Off-peak rates are 75p for adults and 35p for juniors, and holders of a UB40 between the hours of 9.00 a.m. and 12.00 and from 2.00 p.m. to 4.00 p.m.

RESTRICTIONS
Juniors under eighteen must have an authorized user's card unless accompanied by a responsible adult. Authorized user cards are obtained by a 'climbing test' (!)

THE WALL
The wall is self-contained and has rock holds inset. Designed by Don Robinson and built in 1985.

FACILITIES
These include shower and changing rooms, weight training facilities and refreshments.

THE ROTHWELL SPORTS CENTRE (Very Good)
WAKEFIELD ROAD
OULTON
LEEDS LS26 8EL
Telephone: (0532) 824110

The climbing wall is open to the general public, and is found by taking Junction 30 off the M62 (this is the A142) towards Rothwell.

OPENING TIMES
These vary and it is advisable to ring reception to check.

PRICE
The entrance fee is £1.25 for adults and 75p for juniors. Discounts are available on production of a UB40 on weekdays between 9.00 a.m. and 12.00 and 2.00 p.m. and 4.00 p.m.

RESTRICTIONS
Juniors must be supervised.

THE WALL
Incorporated into one end of the sports hall and made from brick. It
was built in 1974 by Don Robinson.
   The nearest major climbing area is the Yorkshire Dales.

OTHER FACILITIES
These include shower, changing and weight training facilities and
refreshments.

DEPT OF PHYSICAL EDUCATION (Very Good)
UNIVERSITY OF LEEDS
LEEDS
YORKSHIRE LS2 9JT
Telephone: (0532) 431 751

The wall is open to the public and is found by first finding the
Parkinson Building (this is a very large building with a square clock
tower) on Woodhouse Lane, the road to Otley. Enter the university
precinct at this point and ask directions to the Students' Union,
the climbing wall is in the P.E. Centre at the back corner of the S.U.
building.

OPENING TIMES
The wall is closed at weekends. It is open during the week between the
hours of 9.00 a.m. and 4.30 p.m. On Tuesdays and Thursdays it is open
from 9.00 a.m. to 8.30 p.m.

PRICE
The entrance fee is 50p.

RESTRICTIONS
None.

FACILITIES
Showers and changing rooms are available.

THE WALL
The wall is sited in a corridor, made from bricks and rocks inset. Built
in 1964 and designed by Don Robinson. This is the first wall to be
adapted for climbing training.
   The nearest crags are Caley, Almscliffe and Ilkley.

THE ALAN ROUSE CLIMBING WALL (Very Good)
SHEFFIELD POLYTECHNIC
COLLEGIATE CRESCENT SITE GYM
BROOMGROVE ROAD
SHEFFIELD S10
Telephone: (0742) 720911 ext 2214, or 665274 ext 3316 for availability

Anyone can use the wall. It is found by taking the A625 Eccleshall Road from the city centre. Broomgrove Road is 1 mile from the centre on the right-hand side.

PRICE
There is no charge.

OPENING TIMES
These vary from term to term but generally the wall is open most evenings throughout the week.

THE WALL
The wall is self-contained and made of concrete block lining and stone. It was opened in 1987 and designed by D. R. Climbing Walls Ltd.

FACILITIES
These include showers up to 4.00 p.m. and changing rooms, weight training facilities and refreshments Monday to Friday.

WEST COMMON SPORTS HALL (Worth a Visit)
WEST COMMON LANE
SCUNTHORPE
SOUTH HUMBERSIDE
Telephone: (0724) 865407

The climbing wall is open to the general public and for eight to twenty-one year olds. Clubs can hire the wall at weekends.

OPENING TIMES
At weekends the wall is open by hire and on Wednesdays and Thursdays between 7.00 p.m. and 10.00 p.m.

PRICE
The entrance fee is 50p for visitors, or through yearly membership. Unemployed persons pay 30p.

RESTRICTIONS
Supervised climbing only, unless used by a club.

THE WALL
Built into one end of the sports hall and made from brick. It was constructed in 1967 and designed by H.C.C.
   The nearest major climbing area is the Peak District.

FACILITIES
All the necessary facilities are available.

THE LOUISA CENTRE (Worth a Visit if Convenient)
FRONT STREET
STANLEY
CO. DURHAM DH8 0TE
Telephone: (0207) 230311

Open to all and found by following the road signs to Stanley Sports Centre. What could be easier?

OPENING TIMES
During the week these are 9.00 a.m. to 10.30 p.m. On Saturdays between 9.00 a.m. and 5.00 p.m. and on Sundays between 9.00 a.m. and 10.30 p.m. The centre is closed on public bank holidays.

PRICE
The entrance fee is two-fold. Admission is 25p per adult and 20p per junior, i.e. under sixteen, and 70p per hour on the wall for an adult and 30p per junior.

RESTRICTIONS
None!

THE WALL
Self-contained, made from natural stone and brick, built in 1979–80 by Mr Robinson of Durham. (Is this the same one I wonder?)
    The nearest climbing area is Causey Arch.

OTHER FACILITIES
Refreshments are available and shower and changing facilities also, weight training facilities too.

CROWTREE CLIMBING WALL (Worth a Visit if Convenient)
CROWTREE LEISURE CENTRE
CROWTREE ROAD
SUNDERLAND SR1 3EL
Telephone: (091) 514 2511

The wall is not open to the general public (see restrictions) and is found from the A1(M) by taking the turn off to Sunderland (A690) and following this road into the town centre, from where Crowtree is signposted.

OPENING TIMES
These are 9.15 a.m. to 11.00 p.m., except during the winter when the centre is closed all day Wednesdays.

PRICE
The entrance fee is 35p for non-member entry, plus the wall fee of 55p (peak) adult and 30p (off-peak). Discounts are available with annual membership of the sports centre and group booking rates. £1.65 off-peak and £3.00 peak.

RESTRICTIONS
These are that club use requires qualified instruction and that individual users are registered. Suitable attire such as EBs and no soloing above 15 feet.

THE WALL
Incorporated into the sports hall walls and of general block construction with stone/belay inserts and concrete handholds, chimney/wall features and ledges. It was built in 1977 and designed by Don Robinson.

OTHER FACILITIES
Weight training, shower and changing, and refreshment facilities are available.

SUNDERLAND OUTDOOR ACTIVITIES ASSOCIATION
(Very Good)
1–3 HIND STREET
SUNDERLAND
SR1 3QD
Telephone: (091) 5657630

The wall is open to the general public and is found by going east along Chester Road toward the centre of Sunderland. At the roundabout at the very end of Chester Road, turn left and follow the one-way system round to the left for 100 yards. The centre is in the large building on the left, with a car park in front on the opposite side of the cobbled road.

OPENING TIMES
Between 9.00 a.m. and 9.00 p.m.

PRICE
The entrance fee is 30p, or £1.00 with instruction, although this has to be booked in advance. For group instruction, it is 75p per head.

RESTRICTIONS
None.

THE WALL
Self-contained and made of bricks with real rock implants. Built originally in 1979 and improved in 1985, the design has 'evolved' over the years. I think we know what that means: chip . . . chip . . .

The nearest climbing areas are Northumberland and the North York Moors.

OTHER FACILITIES
Refreshments are available.

Peak

ACKERS TRUST (Very Good)
GOLDEN HILLOCK ROAD
SMALL HEATH
BIRMINGHAM B11 2PY
Telephone: (021) 771 4448 for bookings and 772 3739 for general enquiries.

The wall is open to the general public and is sited in what used to be the old BSA Social Club on Golden Hillock Road.

OPEN TIMES
At weekends from 9.30 a.m. to 6.30 p.m. and weekdays from 9.00 a.m. to 10.00 p.m.

PRICE
Discounts are available to UB40 holders and members of the Centre.

RESTRICTIONS
Users have to be over 8 years old.

THE WALL
An outdoor construction made from brick and a variety of natural stone, designed by Don Robinson Climbing Walls in 1985.

FACILITIES
Changing, weight training and bar facilities are nearby in the main centre.

COVENTRY SPORTS CENTRE
FAIRFAX STREET
COVENTRY
CV1 5RY
Telephone: (0203) 28601

The climbing wall is open to the general public and is signposted from the city centre ring road.

OPENING TIMES
On Mondays to Sundays between 9.00 a.m. and 10.30 p.m. Under-sixteens must be accompanied by an adult.

PRICE
The fee is 75p per adult, 40p per junior and OAPs, £5.00 for clubs per hour.

RESTRICTIONS
Helmets are compulsory.

THE WALL
Incorporated into one end of the sports hall. It was built in 1975 from brick work with concrete features. The mystery designer strikes again.
   The nearest good crags are in the Peak District.

FACILITIES
Facilities available include weight training and shower/changing, also refreshments.

HUCKNALL LEISURE CENTRE (Very Good)
LINBY ROAD
HUCKNALL
NOTTINGHAM NG15 7TX
Telephone: (0602) 640641. For bookings only, 641333.

The wall is open to everyone and is found either by following the A611 from Nottingham to Hucknall, turn right at the Byron Cinema, then second left into Linby Road where the centre is situated about 300 yards on the left; *or* following the A611 to Nottingham from Junction 27 (M1) into Hucknall past the Market Place on your right. Turn left at Byron Cinema and continue as before. Phew!

OPENING TIMES
This is all pretty complicated, but here goes . . .
   Because the hall is multi-purpose, access is limited. The regular times when climbing is available are as follows:
Tuesdays between 5.00 p.m. and 10.00 p.m.
Wednesdays between 6.00 p.m. and 10.00 p.m. and
Fridays between 6.00 p.m. and 10.00 p.m.
   At other times climbers compete with other sportsmen, using a booking system. Bookings may be made up to seven days in advance by telephone (see above) or by calling at reception from 10.00 a.m. each day. All bookings are provisional until paid for and payment must be made two complete days before the booking date. If the booking isn't paid for by the stated time, the facility is available for a late booking. If I were you, though, I'd just turn up.

PRICE
The fee system is as simple as the booking procedure. Peak rates apply from 5.00 p.m. onwards Monday to Friday and all day Sunday. All

other times are off-peak. For one climber per hour, peak rate is £1.15. Off-peak rates per adult are 95p and for a junior 70p.

Group bookings are £8.05, peak rate, and off-peak £4.85.

RESTRICTIONS
Everyone must sign a disclaimer form. Parental signature required for under-eighteens.

THE WALL
Built at one end of a sports hall, made from granite and limestone set in concrete blocks on engineering brick background. Sounds quite nice. Built in 1984.

The nearest major centre is the Peak District.

OTHER FACILITIES
All the expected facilities are available.

KEELE UNIVERSITY SPORTS CENTRE (Very Good)
KEELE
NR STOKE
STAFFS
Telephone: (0782) 621111 (during the day) and 625313 (after 5.00 p.m.)

The wall is open to the general public.

OPENING TIMES
10.00 a.m. to 10.00 p.m. on weekdays and 10.00 a.m. to 6.00 p.m. at weekends.

PRICE
80p.

RESTRICTIONS
Under 16s must be supervised. An indemnity form must be signed.

THE WALL
Of Bendcrete construction.

HINDLEYS COLLEGE
FOREST STREET
SHEPSHED
LEICESTER LE12 7DB
Telephone: (0509) 504511

The climbing wall is not yet open to members of the public. However, for the time when it is, directions are as follows: leave the

M1 at Junction 23 and take the A512 towards Ashby. At the first set of traffic lights turn right and travel 1 mile to a staggered junction where you turn right into Forest Street. The college is on the right just before a sharp left bend.

OPENING TIMES
The wall is used mainly by groups affiliated to the college, during the evening and weekends. Some casual use occurs during the day when school students are not using it.

PRICE
The cost is £3 (!) per hour for individuals or groups and is bookable through the Vice Principal's office.

RESTRICTIONS
All casual users have to sign an indemnity form. Helmets are compulsory.
    Leaders of school or youth groups have to be approved rock climbing leaders within the Leicestershire Education Leaders Scheme, for more details contact The Education Advisory Dept at County Hall, Glenfield, Leicester.

THE WALL
The wall is in a purpose-built room which is lockable, and is made from breeze blocks and granite blocks set into concrete, moulded concrete holds with inset pegs and belay points. It was built in 1976 and designed by Mike Josie who was advisor for outdoor activities in Leicestershire.
    The nearest crags are Outwoods Crag at Loughborough or Beacon Hill near Loughborough or the good old Peak District.

FACILITIES
These include shower/changing rooms, refreshments and weight training facilities in the main centre.

MOAT COMMUNITY COLLEGE (Worth a Visit)
MAIDSTONE ROAD
LEICESTER LE2 0TU
Telephone: (0533) 25705

The climbing wall is open to the general public and directions from Leicester B.R. station are as follows: go left down Conduit Street, turn right, then immediately left down Maidstone Road. The college is approximately 200 yards on the left.

OPENING TIMES
The wall must be booked in advance through the Community office.

Times are between 9.00 a.m. and 9.00 p.m., except for the last two weeks in August.

PRICE
At weekends this is £1.00 per 1½ hour session for an individual and 75p during the week. For adult groups (C.C.?), weekdays cost £3.75 and weekends £4.50. For youth groups weekday charges are £2.25 and £3.00 at the weekends. For school groups weekday charges are £1.50 and weekends are £2.25. Crikey!
   (And now for the . . .)

RESTRICTIONS
(Here goes)
There must always be two or more climbers within the wall.
Helmets are obligatory for the under-eighteens.
Soloing above 10–12 feet is not allowed.
Under-eighteens must be supervised.
Maximum of twenty people at one time.
No chipping or cutting holes, tsch, tsch, naughty, naughty . . .
The door to the wall should be kept locked during each session. (This must be so that you can't escape until you've got a pump on.)
Etc. Etc.

THE WALL
Self-contained, made from breeze blocks and stone. Built in 1981.
   The nearest good crags are in the Peak District.

FACILITIES
Facilities available include weight training and shower/changing rooms. Refreshments are only available between 7.30 p.m. and 8.30 p.m. at the present time.

REDDITCH YOUTH AND COMMUNITY CENTRE
(Worth a Visit if Convenient)
IPSLEY STREET
REDDITCH
WORCS B98 7AR
Telephone: (0527) 63821

The wall is open to the general public and is found by following the signs to the town centre, turning left at the roundabout before the ring road into Otter Road. Turn right into Ipsley Street and the centre is approximately 400 yards on the left.

OPENING TIMES
Mondays, Wednesdays and Fridays between 7.30 p.m. and 10.00 p.m., Fridays also between 11.00 a.m. and 4.00 p.m. Sundays from 6.30 p.m. to 9.00 p.m.

PRICE
The entrance fee is 50p and discounts are available, with annual membership of 75p for under-eighteens and £1.50 for the over-eighteens. The entrance fee is then reduced to 20p for under-eighteens and 35p for over-eighteens.

RESTRICTIONS
An instructor has to be on duty unless you are an experienced climber, which is all of us, right?

THE WALL
Built at one end of a sports hall, made from concrete brick and wood. Built in 1969, of unknown design.
    The nearest major climbing area is Symonds Yat or Cheddar.

OTHER FACILITIES
All facilities, such as weight training, shower and changing, and refreshments, are at hand. ·

Wales

PLAS MENAI NATIONAL WATERSPORTS CENTRE (Very Good)
CAERNARFON
GWYNEDD LL55 1VE
Telephone: (0248) 670964

The climbing wall is open to the general public and is signposted from the main Caernarfon to Bangor Road.

OPENING TIMES
These are from 9.00 a.m. to 10.00 p.m. Groups must book in advance.

PRICE
The entrance fee is 80p per session or £30 for a season ticket.

RESTRICTIONS
Groups under instruction must wear helmets and use ropes. Individual climbers use the wall at their own risk.

THE WALL
Self-contained, made from natural stone, mainly granite, and designed by John Jackson in 1983.
    The nearest real stuff is Snowdonia.

OTHER FACILITIES
Refreshments are available and shower and changing facilities also.
    A visit here is a real pleasure!

PLAS Y BRENIN (Very Good)
CAPEL CURIG
BETWS Y COED
NORTH WALES
Telephone: (06904) 214

The wall is open to the general public and is sited just by the side of the main centre.

OPENING TIMES
The wall is open from 9.00 a.m. to 11.00 p.m. unless it rains and the centre wishes to use the wall for residential courses. It isn't possible to book in advance.

PRICE
There is a charge of 50p for the electricity meter.

THE WALL
The wall is self-contained and has large crash mats which can be pulled away at the last minute to simulate crag conditions. Designed by D.R. Climbing Walls.

FACILITIES
There is a bar which opens about 7.30 p.m.

CHANNEL VIEW SPORTS CENTRE (Very Good)
GYM DRISCOLL WAY
GRANGE TOWN
CARDIFF
Telephone: (0222) 394317

The wall is open to all and is sited off Channel View Road.

OPENING TIMES
The wall is accessible when the centre is open from 11.00 a.m. to 10.00 p.m. every day.

PRICE
£1 and 80p to centre members.

THE WALL
Set apart in a separate room and built by Don Robinson Climbing Walls in 1986.

FACILITIES
All facilities are in the main hall.

223

East Anglia and Home Counties

KELSEY KERRIDGE SPORTS HALL (Very Good)
QUEEN ANNE TERRACE
GONVILLE PLACE
CAMBRIDGE CB1 1NA
Telephone: (0223) 463210

The wall is open to the general public and is found by heading for the centre of Cambridge (Parkers Piece), and the sports hall is between the YMCA and the swimming pool.

OPENING TIMES
Open every day from 9.00 a.m. to 11.00 p.m. There is no indoor wall available between 6.00 p.m. and 8.00 p.m. on Thursdays.

PRICE
Members pay 50p and non-members pay 80p plus 40p for day membership. Discounts are available for UB40 holders.

RESTRICTIONS
On the outside wall, helmets and ropes and a minimum of 2 people are required.
    On the indoor wall, anyone under 18 must have a letter of permission from parents.

THE INDOOR WALL
Sited at one end and side of an ancillary room, built in 1981 by Bendcrete Climbing Walls.

FACILITIES
All the usual sports centre facilities are on offer.

South East

THE UNIVERSITY OF KENT SPORTS CENTRE (Worth a Visit)
CANTERBURY
Telephone: (0227) 764000

The wall is open to the public.

OPENING TIMES
Monday, Tuesday and Wednesday from 9.00 a.m. to 10.00 p.m. Thursday and Friday from 9.00 a.m. to 11.00 p.m. and Saturdays from 9.00 a.m. to 5.30 p.m. Sundays from 2.00 p.m. to 5.30 p.m.
    University activities have priority so it's best to ring to check.

PRICE
£1.50 with discounts existing for members.

THE WALL
Of breeze block construction with real rocks, built by Don Robinson Climbing Walls in 1980.
   The nearest climbing area for Fowlers is Dover.

HATFIELD POLYTECHNIC P.E. DEPT (Worth a Visit)
COLLEGE LANE
HATFIELD
HERTS AL10 9AB
Telephone: (07072) 79461

The wall is accessible to the public (see restrictions).

OPENING TIMES
Individuals can use the wall as members of Herts M.C. or as Associate members of the Polytechnic climbing club between 8.30 p.m. and 10.00 p.m. on Mondays, Tuesdays and Thursdays. Groups can book by prior arrangements. Ring to check.

THE WALL
Built in 1985 by Don Robinson Climbing Walls.

BRIXTON RECREATION CENTRE (Very Good)
BRIXTON
LONDON
Telephone: 01 274 7774

The wall is open to the general public and the nearest tube is Brixton.

OPENING TIMES
The wall is open when the centre is which is from 9.00 a.m. to 10.00 p.m. every day. No access on Wednesdays between 6.00 p.m. and 9.00 p.m.

PRICE
80p per hour with discounts for UB40 holders.

RESTRICTIONS
A limit of 6 people per hour on the wall.

THE WALL
A cramped location in the centre. Built by Don Robinson Climbing Walls in 1986. The wall is quite high and not very wide with plenty of problems nevertheless. Frequented by Dave Cook who will point out problems in a Euro-Communist fashion.

DOWNSIDE SETTLEMENT (Downside & Worth Boys Club)
(Worth a Visit)
COXSON PLACE
DRUID STREET
LONDON SE1 2EZ
Telephone: 01 407 0093/2861

Use of the climbing wall is subject to certain restrictions (see below) and is on Druid Street, on the one-way system going towards London/Tower Bridges.

OPENING TIMES
Facilities are available for hire most weekdays between 9.00 a.m. and 12.00 and 2.00 p.m. and 4,30 p.m. Use of all the club's facilities is restricted to club members in the evenings.

PRICE
The entrance fee is £1.00 per head per hour. Discounts are negotiable for youth groups, so that rules out the C.C.

RESTRICTIONS
None.

THE WALL
Built into one end of the sports hall and made from reinforced concrete. Built in 1980, Bencrete Climbing Walls.

FACILITIES
Shower and changing facilities are available.

IMPERIAL COLLEGE (Worth a Visit)
EXHIBITION ROAD
LONDON SW7
Telephone: 01 589 5111 (general enquiries) or 3500 (students' union)

The nearest tube is South Kensington.

OPENING TIMES
Open all the time to students and staff of the college.

PRICE
Free.

THE WALL
Built in a corridor, of Bendcrete construction and finished in 1976.

THE MICHAEL SOBELL SPORTS CENTRE (Very Good)
HORNSEY ROAD
ISLINGTON
LONDON N7 7NY
Telephone: 01 609 2166

The climbing wall is open to the general public and is close to Finsbury Park Tube Station.

OPENING TIMES
Mondays 8.30 p.m. to 10.30 p.m.
Tuesdays 4.00 p.m. to 10.30 p.m.
Wednesdays 4.00 p.m. to 10.30 p.m.
Thursdays 4.00 p.m. to 10.30 p.m.
Fridays 4.00 p.m. to 10.30 p.m.
Daily open between 12.00 and 2.00 p.m. and during school holidays from 9.00 a.m. to 4.00 p.m. also.

PRICE
The fee is 85p for centre members, otherwise an extra 25p. Discounts are available to UB40 holders.

RESTRICTIONS
None.

THE WALL
Incorporated into one end of the sports hall. Also in a corridor as well. Made from Bendcrete, a mixture of concrete and brick, in 1973/4, designed by Bendcrete Climbing Walls.
   The nearest crags are Harrisons Rocks. There is also a climbing area which is part of an old railway cutting in the Finsbury Park area.

FACILITIES
Facilities available include weight training and shower/changing rooms as well as refreshments.

CLEMENTS HALL SPORTS CENTRE (Worth a Visit)
ROCHFORD
KENT
Telephone: (0702) 207777

The wall is open to the general public.

OPENING TIMES
Access to the climbing wall depends upon other sporting activities so ring to check.

PRICE
For individuals the fee is £1.10 plus 30p entrance. For group bookings it is £6.00 plus the appropriate number of 30p's.

RESTRICTIONS
An indemnity form must be signed. Under 16s are not allowed.

THE WALL
Of blockwork design and built by Don Robinson in 1985.

BRUNEL UNIVERSITY CLIMBING WALL (Very Good)
THE SPORTS CENTRE
BRUNEL UNIVERSITY
UXBRIDGE
MIDDLESEX UB8 3PA
Telephone: (0895) 52361

The wall is open to the general public and the university campus is off Kingston Lane which is off the main Uxbridge/London road A4020. Using the underground means taking the Metropolitan or Piccadilly line to Uxbridge. The bus services are the 204 and 223 from Uxbridge or the 207 from West London.

OPENING TIMES
Monday to Friday 9.30 a.m. to 10.30 p.m.
Saturday 9.30 a.m. to 6.00 p.m.
Sunday 9.30 a.m. to 8.30 p.m.

PRICE
Adults are £1 and juniors are 50p with no discounts.

RESTRICTIONS
These include signing a code of practice and groups must be under instruction.

FACILITIES
All the usual facilities are on hand.

THE WALL
Self-contained but not purpose built, as a separate entity at one end of the sports hall. Originally made in 1972 from natural rock there have been subsequent substantial alterations in 1983, 1984 and 1986, it now contains Bendcrete sections. Designed by Mike Brightwell, Director of Physical Education and Bendcrete Climbing Walls.

South West

YMCA (Worth a Visit)
101–104 WELLS ROAD
TOTTERDOWN
BRISTOL
Telephone: (0272) 775343

The wall is open to the public.

OPENING TIMES
Monday to Friday from 9.00 a.m. to 10.00 p.m.
Saturdays from 9.00 a.m. to noon.
Sundays from 9.00 a.m. to 12.30 p.m.

PRICE
90p.

THE WALL
There are two walls, one for block bookings and one for individuals.
Doctored by local climbers over a period of time.
    The nearest climbing is in the Avon Gorge.

EXMOUTH ROYAL MARINE COMMANDO TRAINING CENTRE
EXMOUTH

The wall isn't open to the general public but members of Exeter
University have access and it's a large club. No ruskies.

OPENING TIMES/PRICE/etc.
Subject to Exeter University M.C.

THE WALL
A high corridor, built by Don Robinson Climbing Walls in 1978.

FERNDOWN SPORTS CENTRE (Worth a Visit)
CHERRY GROVE
FERNDOWN
NR BOURNEMOUTH BH22 9EZ
Telephone: (0202) 877468

The climbing wall is open to the public and is situated off Church Road
between the A31 and A348, and signposted 'Upper School and Sports
Centre' on Church Road.

OPENING TIMES
The wall is open from 8.30 p.m. to 10.30 p.m. on Mondays, 6.30 p.m. to
8.00 p.m. on Tuesdays, 8.30 p.m. to 10.30 p.m. on Wednesdays. At
weekends, it is bookable on the day.

PRICE
The cost is £1 for non-members and 70p for members.

RESTRICTIONS
None.

THE WALL
The wall is incorporated into one end of a sports hall and is in two distinct sections. One part was originally constructed when the sports hall was built in 1976, and designed by the county architect, made of brick and concrete blocks approximately one-third of the hall width. The second part, built in 1986, and designed by members of Wessex Mountaineering Club, is made of natural stone set into a flat brick wall approximately two-thirds of the hall width.

The nearest climbing area is at Swanage on the Dorset coast.

FACILITIES
These include shower/changing rooms, refreshments and weight training facilities.

THE MARJON (COLLEGE OF ST MARK AND ST JOHN)
COMMUNITY SPORT CENTRE (Worth a Visit)
DERRIFORD ROAD
PLYMOUTH PL6 8BH
Telephone: (0752) 790033 or 777188

Our man in the South West reports that the teachers' training college has a new climbing wall reputed to be worth a visit.

OPENING TIMES
Officially the wall is open to climbers on Wednesday evenings from 7.00 p.m. to 9.00 p.m. and Sunday afternoons from 12.00 to 3.00 p.m. Comments such as 'Unfortunately it is sited on the end wall of an indoor gymnasium and every time I've tried to use it there has been a badminton match and climbing has been banned for fear of squashing a player.'

PRICE
50p.

THE WALL
Doctored in 1986 by a local climber to give a good facility.

THE LINK CENTRE (Very Good)
SWINDON
Telephone: (0793) 871111

The wall is open to the general public.

OPENING TIMES
From 8.30 a.m. to 10.30 p.m. subject to minor restrictions.

PRICE
£1.10 for 55 minutes for individuals and £6.50 for group bookings. Discounts are available to UB40 holders making the cost 25p.

THE WALL
The wall has a movable section which tilts about 10%, which sounds a bit worrying. Built by Bendcrete Climbing Walls in 1985.

FACILITIES
All the usual facilities are at hand.

TAUNTON SCHOOL (Worth a Visit)
TAUNTON
SOMERSET TA2 6AD
Telephone: (0823) 279328

The climbing wall is open to recognized clubs only, using the wall on a long-term hire basis.

OPENING TIMES
See above.

THE WALL
Incorporated into one end of a sports hall, built in 1983 and designed by Don Robinson.
   The nearest climbing areas are Exmoor, Dartmoor and the Mendips.

FACILITIES
These include showers/changing rooms, refreshments and weight training facilities.

COMMUNITY COLLEGE
THE MANSION
FORE STREET
TOTNES
Telephone: (0803) 862020

Fore Street is the main street of Totnes, a one-way system running uphill from the bridge. The Mansion is approximately 200 yards up the hill on the left-hand side.

OPENING TIMES
The more accessible climbing wall in South Devon. The Community College is open most evenings as well as during the day.

PRICE
Groups who wish to book are generally asked to pay a small fee for the key.

THE WALL
A converted fives court, the wall is out of doors, but under a raised roof and therefore sheltered from all but the worst weather. 'This excellent little wall is a popular training venue for local climbers.' The South Devon C.C. for example meet here on Thursday evenings.